Tuq&urausiit

ᑐᖅᖢᕋᐅᓰᑦ

ᐃᓄᐃᑦ ᐃᓚᕇᑐᓯᖕᒋᑦ ᐊᒻᒪ ᐊᑦᑎᖅᑐᐃᔾᔪᓯᖕᒋᑦ

ᐋᖅᑭᒃᓱᖅᑕᐅᔪᑦ
ᐱᑕᓱ ᐊᐅᓚᔾᔪᑦ ᐊᒻᒪ ᓗᐃᔅ
ᖕᓛᕼᐅᖅᑎ

ᑐᑭᓕᐅᖅᑕᐅᔪᖅ
ᐱᑕᓱ ᐊᐅᓚᔾᔪᑦ

ᓴᖅᑭᑕᐅᔪᖅ Inhabit Media Inc.
www.inhabitmedia.com
Inhabit Media Inc. (ᐃᖃᓗᐃᑦ) ᑉ. . Box 11125, ᐃᖃᓗᐃᑦ, ᓄᓇᕗᑦ, X0A 1H0
(Toronto) 146ᐊ Orchard View Blvd., Toronto, Ontario, M4R 1C3

ᓴᖅᑭᑕᐅᓂᖕᒐ ᑮᓇᐅᔭᑎᒍᑦ ᐃᑲᔪᖅᑕᐅᒻᒥᔪᖅ ᐃᓚᖕᒐᓂᒃ ᑲᓇᑕᒥ ᑲᑎᒪᔩᓄᑦ ᑕᑯᒥᓇᖅᑐᓕᐊᓂᓯᒪᔪᓄᑦ.

ᓴᖅᑭᑕᐅᔪᖅ ᑲᓇᑕᒥ.

ᐃᓗᓕᖏᑦ

ᐱᖕᒐᓱᐊᑦ

ᑐᖅ ᓱᕋᐅᔩᑦ

ᐱᒋᐊᕐᓂᖅ

ᐱᓚᔨ ᐊᐅᓚᔾᔪᑦ & ᓗᐃᔅ

ᖁᓛᕼᐅᕐᑎ

ᑐᓱᕋᐅᔩᑦ ᐅᖅᑲᐅᓯᐅᖅᒪᑦ ᐃᓄᐃᑦ ᐊᑐᔫᔾᑦ ᐃᓚᒥᓐᓄᑦ, ᓇᓗᓇᐃᑯᑕᐅᑉᓗᓂ ᐃᓚᒌᖕᓂᑉᑎᓐᓂᒃ ᑭᓇᒌᓂᑉᑎᓐᓂᓪᓗ ᖃᓂᔮᑎᒋᕚᓕᕈᑎᒋᑉᓗᒍᓗ. ᐃᓄᐃᑦ ᐊᑐᔪᖕᒪᑕ ᑐᖅᓱᕋᐅᓯᕐᒥᒃ ᐅᐱᒍᓱᒍᑎᐅᕚᓕᖅᓱᓂᓗ ᖃᓂᓪᓕᕚᓕᕈᑕᐅᖕᒪᑦ ᐃᓚᒌᒃᑐᓄᑦ. ᐊᑎᖅᑐᐃᓂᖅ ᐃᓚᑉᑕ ᐊᑏᓂᒃ ᐆᒪᑎᑦᑎᖕᒪᑦ ᐱᕚᑦᓕᕈᑕᐅᖕᒃᓱᓂᓗ ᐱᓕᕆᖅᑎᒌᑦᑎᐊᕐᓂᕐᒥᒃ ᐊᒃᓱᕈᓇᓕᕌᖓᑦ. ᑐᖅᓱᕋᐅᔩᑦ ᐃᑲᔫᕐᓂᖅᑲᓇᕗᖅ ᓄᓇᓕᖕᓄᑦ ᐱᑦᑎᐊᖅᑐᕋᐅᕚᓕᕈᑕᐅᑉᓗᓂ, ᐱᕋᔅᓗᐊᖕᒋᔾᔪᑕᐅᑉᓗᓂ ᖃᓄᖕᒐᓴᓗᐊᙱᕚᓕᕈᑕᐅᑉᓗᓂᓗ.

ᑭᓯᐊᓂ,ᐃᓕᖅᑯᓯᖅ ᑐᖅᓱᕐᓂᖅ ᐱᐊᓚᔪᒥᒃ ᑕᒻᒪᖅᐸᑦᓕᐊᖕᒪᑦ. ᐃᓄᐃᑦ ᓄᓇᓕᖕᒥᓐᓂ ᐅᑉᓗᒥᐅᓕᖅᑐᖅ ᐃᓚᒃᑭᑐᕋᐅᕙᓕᖅᒪᑕ ᖃᑉᓗᓈᑐᑦ ᐊᑎᖅᒥᑎᒍᑦ, ᑐᖅᓱᕋᕈᓯᖅᑲᑐᖕᒋᓱᒍ.

ᑕᒪᔅᓴ ᐃᓚᖓ ᐱᔾᔪᑕᐅᔪᖅ ᖃᓂᑐᕋᐅᔪᓐᓇᐃᐹᓕᕈᑕᐅᔪᖅ ᐃᓚᒌᑐᓂ.

ᑕᒪᓐᓇ ᐱᔾᔪᑎᒋᐸᑐᒍ ᐱᓴᓇᐊᖅᑲᑦᓚᓇᓕᖅᐳᒍᑦ ᓂᐱᓕᐅᓇᓗᑕ ᖃᐅᔨᒪᔪᓂᒃ ᐱᑕᖃᕈᓐᓇᐃᐸᑦᓕᐊᒪᑕ ᐃᓕᖅᑯᓯᐅᓚᐅᖅᑐᓂᒃ ᑐᖅᓱᕋᐅᓯᕐᓂᒃ ᐊᒻᒪ ᐊᑎᖅᑐᐃᓂᕐᒥᒃ. ᖃᐅᔨᒪᔪᓂᒃ ᓂᐱᓕᐅᓇᖕᒋᑉᑯᑉᑕ- ᑐᐊᕕᕐᓗᑕ- ᑕᒻᒪᕐᓂᐊᓕᕐᒪᑕ ᐳᐃᒍᖅᑕᐅᓗᑎᒃᓗ.ᖃᐅᔨᒪᓂᖕᒋᑦ ᐃᓐᓇᐃᑦᑎᑎᕋᖅᑕᐅᓴᓇᐊᖅᑲᓕᕐᒪᑕ ᖃᐅᔨᒪᓴᐅᓕᖅᐸᑦᓕᐊᓂᐊᕐᒪᑕ ᑭᖑᖐᓇᓴᐅᔪᓄᑦ.

ᑖᒻᓇ ᐅᖅᑲᓕᒦᒐᖅ ᐊᐱᖅᓱᕐᓂᑰᖕᒪᑦ ᐃᓐᓇᓇᓴᐅᔪᓂᒃ ᐊᕐᕕᐊᓂ,ᐊᐱᖅᓱᑕᐅᓚᐅᕐᒪᑕ ᑐᖅᓱᕋᐅᓯᕐᓂᒃ ᐊᒻᒪ ᐊᑦᑎᖅᑐᐃᓂᕐᒥᒃ ᑭᙵᑦᓕᕐᒥ, ᑕᓴᒪᓂᖅᓯᐹᒍᑉᓗᑎᒃ ᑭᑎᑉᑎᓂ ᓄᓇᕗᒥᐅᓂ. ᐱᒻᒪᕆᐅᓂᖓ ᖃᐅᔨᒪᓴᐅᓴᕆᐊᖅᑲᖅᓂᖓ ᐱᒻᒪᕆᐅᓗᐊᕐᒪᑦ. ᑭᓇᐅᓂᑉᑎᓐᓂᒃ ᖃᐅᔨᒪᓂᖅᑲᔪᕈᓐᓇᐃᕈᑕᐅᙳᒪᑦ ᐃᓅᓯᕐᒥ.

ᑕᐃᒪᑐᖅ ᑖᒻᓇ ᐅᖅᑲᓕᒦᒐᖅ ᐃᑲᔫᑎᖃᕐᓂᐊᖅᐳᖅ ᒪᑯᖕᓂᕐᓴᓄᑦ ᐃᓕᕐᑯᓯᐅᓚᐅᖅᑐᖅ ᑐᖅᓱᕋᓂᖅ ᑕᒻᒪᕐᑯᓇᒍ.

ᑐᖅᓱᕋᐅᓰᑦ

ᓯᕗᓪᓕᖅᐹᖅ
ᐱᖅᑯᓯᖅᐳᑦ
ᐊᑦᑎᖅᑐᐃᓂᕐᒥᒃ

ᔭᐃᒥᓯ ᑯᓐᓂ
ᐊᐱᖅᓱᖅᑕᐅᒻᒪᑦ ᐅᑉᓗᐊ
ᒪᓐᓃᑦ 2012

ᐊ. ᐅᖃᐅᑎᔫᑦᓗᐊᖅᐱᖕᒐ ᖃᓄᖅ ᐊᑦᑎᖅᑐᐃᓯᒪᖕᒑᑖ?

ᑭ. ᓄᑕᕋᓛᒥᒃ ᐊᑦᑎᕐᓂᑐᓂ ᑭᑐᒥᐊᓂᒃ ᐊᑦᑎᖅᑐᒥᐊᖕᒋᑦᓗᒍ. ᐃᓚᒋᔭᕐᓂᒃ ᐃᓐᓇᓂᒃ ᓯᕗᓪᓕᐅᓗᑎᑦ ᐊᑦᑎᕐᓂᒋᐊᖃᖅᑐᑎᑦ ᐊᑖᑦᑖᖅᑎᓐᓂᒃ,

ᐊᓈᑦᑖᖅᑎᓐᓂᒃ, ᐊᒻᒪ ᐊᖓᔪᖅᑳᕐᓂᒃ. ᐅᐸᓗᒥᐅᑕᖅ ᓄᑕᕋᕐᒥᓐᓂᒃ ᑭᓗᒥᐊᓂᒃ ᐊᑦᑎᓂᒃᑕᑕᕐᒪᑕ ᐱᑦᑕᐅᑎᔾᔪᒥᐊᒥ'ᓂᒃ. ᑕᒪᓐᓇ ᐱᔾᔪᑕᐅᕐᑲᑕᐅᑕᖅᑐᖅ ᓄᑕᕋᓛᑦ ᐃᓅᓯᖅᑐᑦ ᑐᕐᑯᓚᒃᑭᓐᓇᖅᑕᕈᑎᒋᑕᒪᔾᔪᒃ ᐊᖓᔪᖅᑳᖏᑕ ᐊᑦᑎᕐᒪᔾᔪᒃ ᖃᐅᔨᒪᖏᑕᒥ'ᓂᒡ ᓅᓐᓃᑦ. ᐱᖅᑯᓯᓇᓚᐅᕋᓗᐊᕋᑉᑎᒍ ᐊᑦᑎᕐᓂᐸᒃᖁᑕ ᓄᑕᕋᑉᑎᓂᒃ ᐃᓚᑉᑎᓂᒃ.ᒪᒃᑯᒃᑐᑦ ᐅᐸᓗᒥᐅᑕᖅ ᖃᐅᔨᒪᓗᐊᕈᓐᓇᐃᕐᒪᑕ ᖃᐅᔨᒪᔫᔭᖅᑑᓚᓗᐃᑦ ᓱᓇᓗᒃᑖᓂᒃ. ᑕᒪᓐᓇ ᐊᔾᔭᐅᓗᐊᕈᑎᒋᑕᕐᒪᒍ ᑕᐃᑉᓱᒪᓂᒥᑦ.

ᐊ. ᓄᑕᕋᒥᒡᑕ ᐊᑦᑎᖅᓯᒍᕕᑦ ᑖᒻᓇ ᐊᕝᕚᑕ ᑐᖅᖁᕋᐅᓯᐊᓂᒃ ᐊᑐᕐᓗᓂ ᑐᖅᖁᕋᖅᑕᐅᓇᔭᖅᐸ?

ᑭ. ᑭ. ᒪᒃᑯᒃᑐᑦ ᓄᑕᕋᕐᒥ'ᓂᒃ ᐊᒥᓱᒥᐊᔾᔪᐊᕐᓂᒃ ᐊᑎᓂᒃᑕᓇᐊᖅᑲᖏᒻᒪᑕ. ᐃᓅᓇᐃᑦ ᖃᒪᓂᔾᔪᐊᕐᒥᑦ,ᖃᖏᖅᑰᓂᕐᒥᑦ ᐊᕐᕕᐊᓂᑦᑐ ᖃᐅᔨᒪᔫᔾᔫᒻᒪᑕ ᑭᑐᓂᒃ ᐃᓚᖅᑲᕐᒪᖕᓛᕐᒦᒃ. ᐊᑖᑖᕋᓗᒍᑦ ᐊᓈᑖᕋᓗᒍᑦ ᑭᑐᓂᒃ ᐃᓚᖅᑲᕐᒪᖕᓛᑉᑖ ᖃᐅᔨᒪᑦᑎᐊᓚᐅᕐᒪᑕ ᐃᑲᔫᖅᑑᓗᐊᕐᒪᑎᒍᑦ ᑭᑐᓂᒃ ᐊᑦᑎᓂᓚᔭᕐᒪᖕᓛᑉᑖ. ᐃᓄᓐᓂᐊᖅᑐᑦ ᐊᔾᔨᕖᒥᐊᓂᒃ ᐅᖃᓗᒥᐊᓕᕐᒪᑕ ᐃᓄᓐᓂᐊᖅᑎᑕᐅᑕᖅᖁᑎᒃᑯ ᐃᓄᓐᓂᐊᕐᕕᖕᓂ. ᓄᑕᕋᒥ'ᓂᒃ ᐊᑎᓇᔭᓇᐊᖅᑲᖏᑕᖏ'ᓂᒃ ᐊᑦᑎᕐᓂᒃᑕᓕᕐᒪᑕ ᐃᓚᒋᖏᑕᒥᐊᒥ'ᓂᒃ. ᐱᖅᑯᓯᓇᓚᐅᑉᑎᒍ ᓄᑕᕋᑉᑎᓂᒃ ᐃᓚᑉᑎᓂᒃ ᐊᑦᑎᖅᑐᐃᓂᖅ.

ᓕᐅ ᐃᓐᓇᐅᓂᖅᓴᖅ ᐋᒻᒪᖅ
ᐊᐱᖅᓱᖅᑕᐅᒪᑦ ᐅᑉᓗᐊ
ᓴᒡᒋᓇᖕᕕᒃ 2012

ᐊ. ᓄᑕᖅᑲᓂᒃ ᐊᑦᑎᖅᑐᐃᓯᒪᕕᑦ? ᖃᓄᖅ ᐅᖃᐅᑎᔫᓗᐊᖅᐱᙵ ᐱᖅᑯᓯᕐᒥᒃ ᐊᑦᑐᐃᓂᕐᒥᒃ?

ᑭ. ᓄᑕᕋᓗᒃᑖᕗᑦ ᐅᑉᓗᒥ ᐊᑎᖅᑲᓗᒃᑖᖅᑐᑦ ᐃᓐᓇᕆᓚᐅᒐᑉᑎᓂᒃ ᓯᕗᓕᑉᑎᓂᒃ.

ᐊ. ᐊᑦᑎᓯᔪᓂ ᓄᑕᕋᕐᒥᒃ—ᑖᒻᓇ ᓄᑕᕋᖅ ᑐᖅᓱᕋᐅᓯᐊᓂᒃ ᐊᑎᕆᓚᐅᒑᑕ ᑐᖅᓱᕋᖅᑕᐅᓇᔭᖅᐹ?

ᑭ. ᐄ, ᐃᓄᐃᑦ ᐃᓚᖏᑦ ᑐᖅᓱᕋᐅᓯᐅᔪᓂᒃ ᐊᑏᑕ ᑐᖅᓱᕋᖅᑕᐅᓱᖅᑐᑦ, ᐊᒻᒪᑕᐅᖅ ᐃᓚᖏᑦ ᐊᑦᑎᕋᐅᓯᕐᒥᓂᒃ ᐊᑐᖅᓱᑎᒃ ᓄᑕᕋᑉᑎᓄᒃ ᓇᒡᓕᒍᓯᓗᐊᒧᑦ ᐊᑦᑎᕋᐅᓯᑖᖅᑎᑦᑎᓯᕋᑉᑕ. ᐃᓚᖏᑦ ᐊᖓᔪᖅᑳᖏᑕ ᐊᑦᑎᕋᐅᓯᑖᑎᓐᓂᑯᐃᓂᒃ ᐊᑎᖅᑲᒥᐊᔪᔪᑦ. ᐃᓚᖏᑦ ᐊᖓᔪᖅᑳᑦ ᓴᑭᖏᑕ ᐊᑏᓂᒃ ᓇᒡᓕᒍᓯᖕᓂᖅᓴᐅᕙᖕᒪᑕ ᐊᖓᔪᖅᑳᖏᓐᓂᒃ ᐊᑦᑎᖅᓯᒪᔪᓂᒃ ᓇᒡᓕᒍᓯᖏᓂᖅᓴᐅᑉᓗᑎᒃ. ᑕᒪᓐᓇ ᐃᓕᖅᑯᓯᕆᓚᐅᕋᑉᑎᒍ.

ᐊ. ᑖᒻᓇᓕ ᐊᕝᕙᕆᔭᐅᔪᖅ ᐱᑦᑎᐊᑕᐅᕚᓪᓕᖅᐸᓚᐅᖅᐸᑦ ᐊᑎᐊ ᐱᔾᔪᑕᐅᕝᔪᓃ?

ᑭ. ᑎᐊ'ᐊᐃᐸᒃᑐᑦ ᐃᓄᐃᑦ ᓄᑕᕋᖅ ᐊᑎᖅᑲᕌᖓᑦ ᑕᐃᒃᓱᒥᖓ ᐅᐱᒋᔭᖓᓂᒃ; ᐊᖓᔪᖅᑳᖏᑦ ᐅᐱᒋᔭᐅᓕᖅᐹᓕᖅᐸᒃᑐᑦ. ᐃᓚᖏᑦ ᐊᑦᑎᕋᐅᓯᕐᓂᒃ ᐊᑐᖅᐸᒃᑐᑦ ᐃᓄᖕᓄᑦ ᐊᑐᒐᐅᒥᐊᓕᖅᓱᓂ, ᐃᓚᖏᑦᑕᐅᖅ

ᐊᑎᓪᓗᐊᕙᖕᒥᓐᓂᒃ ᐊᑐᖅᐸᒃᑑᒐᓗᐃᑦ. ᐃᓄᐃᑦ ᐅᖃᐅᓯᖏᑦ ᐊᔾᔨᒌᖏᒪᑕ ᐃᓕᖏᑉᑕᐅᖅ ᓇᐃᑐᓈᓂᒃ ᐊᑦᑎᖅᑕᐅᙳᒪᑕ.

ᐊ. ᐅᐱᒋᔭᐅᕚᓪᓕᕈᑎᒋᕙᐅᒃ ᐊᑦᑎᑐᐃᖅᑲᑕᐅᑕᑕᓕᖅᕙᑦ ᓄᓇᓕᑉᓯᓐᓂᑦ?

ᑭ. ᐄ,ᓄᑕᕋᖅᑲᕋᑉᑕ ᐊᒥᓱᓂᒃ.ᑎᒍᐊᖅᑲᖅᑐᑕᓗ ᐊᒻᒪ ᓇᒡᒥᓂᖅ ᓄᑕᕋᖅᑲᖅᑐᑕ. ᑖᒃᑯᐊ ᓇᓗᓇᐃᒃᑯᑕᐅᕗᑦ ᐅᐱᒍᓱᖕᒪᑕ ᐃᓅᓯᕆᔭᑉᑎᓐᓂᓪᓗ ᐊᑐᕐᓂᖅᑲᑦᑎᐊᖅᑐᑎᒃ. ᐃᓄᐃᑦ ᑐᓂᓯᕗᖕᒪᑕ ᓄᑕᖅᑲᓂᒃ ᐊᖕᒐᔪᖅᑳᑦᑕᐅᓇᓱᒋᔭᕐᒥᓐ ᓄᑦ,ᑐᓂᔭᐅᒐᑉᑕ ᓄᑕᕋᕐᒥᒃ ᐅᐱᒍᓱᓐᓂᐅᓚᐅᕐᒪᑦ.

ᐊ. ᓄᑕᕋᕐᒥᒃ ᐊᑦᑎᕐᓂᒃᑐᓂ ᐃᓅᔪᓐᓇᐃᖅᓯᒪᓕᖅᑐᒥᒃ ᑕᒪᓐᓇ ᐃᑲᔪᕖᓕᕈᑕᐅᕙᒃᐸ ᓴᐃᒪᖅᑎᑦᑎᕖᓕᖅᐸᒃᐹ ᑖᒃᑯᓄᖓ ᐃᓚᐃᓚᐅᖅᑐᓄᑦ?

ᑭ. ᐄ; ᐃᑲᔪᕖᓕᖅᐸᒃᑐᖅ ᐊᓐᓂᐊᓗᐊᕈᓐᓇᐃᕐᓇᕐᒪᑦ ᐃᓅᔪᓐᓇᐃᖅᑐᖅ ᐊᑦᑎᖅᑕᐅᓴᖀᖕᒐᑦ, ᖁᕙᐊᓇᖅᓯᕖᓕᖅᓱᓂᓗ. ᐅᒡᒍᐊᕈᓐᓇᐃᑉᐹᓕᕐᓇᖅᑐᖅ ᖁᕙᐊᓯᓕᖅᐹᓕᕐᓇᖅᓱᓂᓗ ᐊᑎᐊ ᖃᐃᓯᒪᓕᖀᖕᒐᑦ ᐅᕝᕙᒍᑎᔭᕐᒥ. ᐃᓚᖕᒋᐊᓖᑦ ᐅᖃᖕᒪᑕ, "ᓴᐃᒻᒪᕖᓕᖅᐳᖕᒐ ᐅᑎᖅᑭᒪᓕᕐᒪᑦ ᐅᕙᑉᑎᓄᑦ ᓇᒡᓕᒋᓚᐅᒐᕐᔪᐊᓇᒐᑉᑯ." ᑎᐊ'ᐊ ᐃᓄᐃᑦ ᐃᓚᖏ ᐅᖃᖕᒪᑕ ᐃᓚᒋᓚᐅᖅᑕᒥᓐᓂᒃ ᐊᑦᑎᓂᑲᓐᓂᖀᖕᒐᒥᒃ.

ᐊ. ᐅᑉᓗᒥᐅᓕᖅᑐᕐᑕ ᑐᖅᓱᕋᐅᔩᑦ ᐊᔾᔭᐅᓕᖅᐸᑦ?

ᑭ. ᓇᐅᒃ, ᐊᐅᓚᓵᓕᕋᒪᓗᒃᑖᖅ ᑐᖅᓱᕋᕐᓂᖅ ᐊᔾᔭᕈᖕᒋᑐᖅ ᓱᓕ ᐊᑐᕋᑉᑎᒍ ᐅᑭᐅᓄᑦ ᐊᒥᓱᕐᔪᐊᕐᓄᑦ. ᐊᔾᔭᕈᖅᑐᓂᒃ ᐅᔾᔨᕈᓱᖕᒋᑦᑐᖕᒐ ᑐᖅᓱᕋᐅᓯᕐᓂᒃ ᐃᓅᖅᑲᑎᓪᓂ.

ᐊ. ᖃᓄᕐᓕ ᐊᑦᑎᖅᑐᐃᓂᖅ ᓄᑕᕋᒥᒃ ᐊᑐᖅᑎᒋᕙ?

ᑭ. ᐊᑐᖅᑐᔾᔪᐊᖅ, ᑭᑐᓂᒃ ᐃᓚᖃᕐᒪᖔᑉᑖ ᖃᐅᔨᒪᕚᓪᓕᕈᑎᒋᕙᒃᑲᑉᑎᒍ. ᐃᓅᖅᑲᑎᑉᑎᓂᖕᓄ ᑭᑐᓂᒃ ᐃᓚᖃᕐᒪᖔᑖ ᖃᐅᔨᒪᔾᔪᑎᒋᕙᒃᓱᒋᑦ, ᐊᑐᕐᓂᓕᒃ ᐊᑦᑎᖅᑐᐃᓂᖅ ᐃᓚᑉᑎᓂᒃ.

ᐊ. ᑕᐃᑉᓱᒪᓂᓕ ᐊᑦᑎᖅᑐᐃᓂᕐᒧ ᑐᖅᓱᕋᕐᓂᕐᒧ ᐊᑐᖅᑕᐅᑦᑎᐊᓚᐅᖅᐸ?

ᑭ. ᐄ, ᑕᐃᑉᓱᒪᓂ ᐃᓄᒃᑐᐃᓐᓇᖅ ᐊᑎᖅᐳᑦ ᐊᑐᖅᐸᓚᐅᕋᑉᑎᒍ ᐃᓅᓰᖅᑎᓪᓗᑕ ᐊᑦᑎᖅᑕᐅᓂᑯᕗᑦ. ᐅᑉᓗᒥ ᓱᓕ ᐊᑐᖅᑕᐅᕙᒃᑑᓚᓗᐊᖅ ᐃᓄᐃᑦ ᐃᓚᖏᓐᓄᑦ ᐃᓄᒃᑐᑦ atianik ᐊᑐᒥᐊᔪᔪᑦᓱᓕ; ᐃᓚᒌᑎᒍᑦ ᑐᓱᕋᖅᑐᕋᐅᐸᒃᑲᑉᑕ ᓱᓕ.

ᐊ. ᐊᑦᑎᖅᓯᓂᖅ ᐊᒃᑐᐃᓂᖃᖅᐹ ᐊᕝᕙᓇᔭᐅᔪᒧᑦ?

ᑭ. ᐄ; ᓄᑕᕋᓛᖅ ᐊᑦᑎᖅᑕᐅᐸᑦ ᐃᓐᓇᐅᑉ ᐊᑎᐊᓂᒃ, ᑖᒪ ᐊᑦᑎᖅᑕᐅᔪᖅ ᐃᓐᓇᖅ ᐅᖅᑲᖅᐸᑦ ᐊᕝᕙᕐᒥᓄᑦ ᐃᓅᓰᖅᑎᓗᒍ ᓄᑕᕋᖅ ᐅᖅᑲᐅᓯᐅᓚᐅᖅᑐᒥᒃ ᐃᓅᓯᖅᑲᓪᓕᓯᕐᒪᑦ ᐃᓐᓇᐅᑉ ᐅᖅᑲᐅᓯᐊ ᐱᓪᒍᔪᔾᔫᒻᒪᑦ. ᑕᒪᓐᓇᐱᓪᓗᐊᕕᔪᖕᒪᑦ. ᓄᑕᕋᓛᖅ ᑐᑭᓯᐊᖕᒋᒃᑲᓗᐊᕐᓗᓂ ᐃᓅᓯᖅᑲᓪᓕᓯᕐᒪᕐᑦ ᐅᖅᑲᐅᓯᐅᔪᒥᒃ.

ᐊ. ᑐᖅᓱᕋᕐᓂᖅ ᐊᔾᔨᒌᖕᒋᐸ ᐃᓄᖕᓄᑦ ᐃᓚᒌᖕᒋᑐᓄᑦ?

ᑭ. ᐄ; ᐊᔾᔨᒌᖕᒋᑦᑐᖅ ᓄᓇᓖᑦ ᐅᖅᑲᐅᓯᖕᖑᑦ ᐊᔾᔨᒌᖕᒋᒻᒪᑦ. ᐊᖅᕕᐊᖅᒥᐅᑕᐅᓪᓚ ᑐᖅᓱᕋᐅᓯᕋ ᐊᔾᔨᒋᖕᒋᒻᒪᒍᑦ ᐅᖅᑲᐅᓯᕗᑦ ᐊᔾᔨᒌᖕᒋᒻᒪᑦ.

ᒪᑎᐅᑕ ᓱᓗᕌᔮᒃ
ᐊᐱᖅᓱᖅᑕᐅᒪᑦ ᐅᐸᓗᐊ
ᓴᒡᒋᓇᖕᕚᒃ 2012

ᐊ. ᐅᖃᐅᑎᔩᑦᓗᐊᖅᐱᖕᒐ ᖃᓄᖅ ᐊᑦᑎᖅᑐᐃᓱᒪᖕᒑᑖ?

ᑭ. ᐊᖕᒐᔪᒃᑖᑦ ᓄᑕᕋᖅᑲ ᐊᑦᑎᖅᑕᐅᓚᐅᖅᒪᑕ ᐊᓈᓇᒻᓄᑦ.ᐊᓈᓇᒐ ᐃᓅᔪᓐᓇᐃᖅᒪᑦ, ᐊᑦᑎᖅᓯᑦᑕᓕᓚᐅᖅᒪ ᐃᖕᒍᑕᒻᓂᒃ ᐊᒻᒪ ᓄᑲᖅᑲᖅᐹᓂᒃ ᓄᑕᕋᒻᓂᒃ. ᐊᓈᓇᒪ ᐊᖕᒐᔪᒃᑕᖅᐹ ᓄᑕᕋᖅᑖᓇᓴᕋ ᐊᑦᑎᓚᐅᖅᒪᒍ ᑑᑖᒥᒃ,ᐊᒻᒪ ᐊᑦᑎᕋᐅᑎᖃᖅᔪᓂ ᐋᐸᐃᒥᒃ, ᐊᑦᑎᓚᐅᖅᒪᒍ ᐊᐃᒋᓚᐅᖅᑕᕋ ᐃᐱᓚᐅᖅᑐᖅ. ᒪᒃᑯᒃᔪᓂ ᓇᓗᑲᑖᓇᐊᓚᐅᖅᒪᑕ ᐱᖃᑎᖃᖅᔪᓂ ᐱᖕᒐᓱᓂᒃ ᐃᐱᓚᐅᖅᒪᑦ. ᐊᑖᑕᒐ ᐊᑦᑎᕈᐊᓚᐅᕋᑉᑯ ᐊᖅᓇᐅᓗᒍ, ᑕᖃᐃᓯᖅᑯᑉᓗᒍ ᐊᒃᓱᕈᖅᓂᓇᓚᐅᖅᑖᓂᒃ ᐃᓚᒋᔭᖕᒋᑦ ᐱᔾᔦᑎᒋᑉᓗᒋᑦ. ᑕᐃᑉᓱᒪᓂ ᓱᓇᖅᑲᓗᐊᓚᐅᖕᒋᒻᒪᑦ—ᒪᖃᐃᔾᔦᑎᓂᒃ ᓄᓇᒥᐅᑕᐅᖁᑎᑦᓗᑕ. ᐊᖑᑎᑦ ᒪᖃᐃᐸᓚᐅᖅᒪᑕ ᕿᒧᒃᓯᖅᑐᑎᒃ ᐃᑖᓐᓂᑯᑦ ᐱᓱᒃᑐᑎᒃ ᐅᖕᒐᕗᓄᑦ.ᐳᐃᒍᖅᓂᖅ ᐊᔦᓕᓚᐅᕋᑉᑯ ᖃᓄᖅ ᐊᒃᓱᐹᑎᒋᕙᓚᐅᖅᒪᖕᒑᑎᒍᑦ ᐊᓐᓇᒃᑎᓐᓂᓗᒃᑐᑕ,ᐸᓂᒋᔦᒪᓕᓚᐅᕋᑉᑯ.

ᓯᑕᒪᐃᓐᓇᓂᒃ ᓇᖕᒥᓂᖅ ᓄᑕᖃᖅᑲᖃᒪ. ᐹᓯᒥᒃ ᓄᑕᕋᖅᑖᕋ ᐊᓈᓇᒐ ᐅᖅᑲᓗᒡᕕᒋᓚᐅᕋᑉᑯ ᐃᓅᓵᖅᑎᑦᓗᒍ. ᐊᓈᓇᒪ ᐊᐱᓇᓚᐅᖅᒪᖔ, “ᐸᓂᒃᑖᕐᓂᖁᕕᑦ ᑭᓇᒥᒃ ᐊᑎᕐᑲᕐᓂᐊᐸ?” ᐅᖅᑲᐅᑎᑉᓗᒍ, “ᐸᓂᒃᑖᖅᑐᖕᒐ, ᒪᖃᐃᑕᕐᓂᐊᖕᒋᓕᕐᒪᑦ ᓂᕐᑭᒃᓴᓯᐅᖅᑕᖕᒋᓛᕐᓗᓂ ᐱᓕᓇᕐᔪᐊᑕᕐᓂᐊᖕᒋᓕᕐᒪᑦ ᐊᑦᑎᕐᓂᐊᖅᑕᕋ ᐊᑖᑕᒻᓂᒃ. ᖃᓄᕐᑖᓱᒪᒋᕕᐅᒃ?” ᑭᐅᓚᐅᖅᑐᖅ, “ᐄ ᓈᒪᒃᑐᖅ.” ᑕᐃᒪ ᐸᓂᒐ ᐊᑖᑕᒻᓂᒃ ᐊᑎᖃᓕᖅᐳᖅ, ᐃᓴᒃᑭᐊᕐᒥᒃ.

ᔩᑎ ᐃᓅᓚᐅᖅᐳᖅ ᐹᓯ ᐱᖕᒐᓱᓂᒃ ᐅᑭᐅᖃᖅᑎᑦᓗᒍ. ᔩᑎ ᓴᑭᒪ ᐊᑎᓚᐅᖅᒪᒍ. ᓴᑭᒐ ᐊᑎᖃᓚᐅᖅᒪᑦ ᐅᔭᕋᑖᕐᒥᒃ, ᓇᐅᔮᑉ ᓄᓕᐊᓇᓚᐅᒑ. ᔩᑎ ᐊᑎᖃᖅᒪᑦ ᓯᐅᑦᑐᖕᒥᒃ, ᓴᑭᒪ ᐊᐃᕕᓂᐊᓂᒃ ᐊᑎᖃᖅᒪᑦ. ᓄᑕᕋᖅᑖᓇᓯᒪᔭᑐᒃᑖᒻᓂᑦ ᐹᓯᑐ ᔩᑎᑐ ᐊᑦᑎᖅᓯᒪᔭᑐᐊᓇᒐᑉᑭᒃ. ᐱᖕᒐᓱᓂᒃ ᓄᑕᕋᑦᑐᐊᕕᖃᕋᒪ, ᐹᓯᑐ, ᔩᑎᑐ ᐃᕐᓂᕋᑐ, ᑖᒻᓇ ᓯᑕᒪᖕᒐᑦ ᓄᑲᖅᑲᐹᖕᒍᓚᐅᖅᑐᖅ ᑎᒍᐊᖕᒍᓚᐅᖅᒪᑦ ᑲᖕᒋᖅᑲᓂᕐᒥᐅᑕᕐᓄᑦ ᒫᓇ

ᑎᑭᕋᕐᔪᐊᕐᒥᐅᑕᐅᓕᖅᑐᓄᑦ. ᐅᓴᒃᑯᑦ ᑎᒍᐊᕆᓚᐅᕐᒪᔾᔪᒃ ᐃᕐᓂᖅᐳᑦ ᓄᑲᖅᓯᐹᖅ.

ᑐᒃᓯᓇᓚᐅᕐᒪᒍ ᐃᕐᓂᑐᐊᓇᔭᑉᑕ, ᑐᓂᔪᒪᓗᐊᓚᐅᖕᒋᑲᓗᐊᕋᑉᑯ. ᑎᒍᐊᖕᒍᓚᐅᕐᒪᑦ ᐊᖕᒐᔪᖅᑳᑉᑕ ᐱᔭᐅᖁᓚᐅᕐᒪᒍ ᐃᓱᒪᑕᐅᓚᐅᕐᒪᑕ ᓄᑕᕋᓇᔭᑉᑎᓐᓄᑦ. ᐊᒥᓲᔾᔪᐊᕐᓂᒃ ᐃᓕᓐᓂᐊᖅᑎᓯᒪᖕᒪᑎᒍᑦ ᐃᓅᓯᕐᒥᒃ ᓄᑕᕋᖃᕐᓂᕐᒥᒡᓗ. ᐃᕐᓂᕋ ᐊᖕᒐᔪᖅᓯᐹ ᓄᑲᖅᑲᓚᐅᖕᒋᒻᒪᑦ ᑐᓂᔪᒪᓚᐅᖕᒋᒃᑲᓗᐊᕋᑉᑯ ᑭᓯᐊᓂ ᐊᓈᓇᒪ ᑎᒍᐊᖕᒍᖁᓚᐅᕐᒪᒍ ᓈᓚᒋᐊᖃᓚᐅᕋᒪ. ᑕᐃᒪᓐᓇ ᐃᓐᓇᕗᑦ ᐊᐅᓚᑦᑎᕙᓚᐅᕐᒪᑕ ᓈᓚᒋᐊᖃᖅᐸᓚᐅᕋᑉᑎᒍ.

ᐊ. ᓄᑕᕋᒥᒡᓕ ᐊᑦᑎᖅᓱᒍᕕᑦ ᑖᒻᓇ ᐊᕝᕚᑕ ᑐᖅᖢᕋᐅᓯᐊᓂᒃ ᐊᑐᕐᓗᓂ ᑐᖅᖢᕋᖅᑕᐅᓇᔭᖅᐸ?

ᑭ. ᐄ, ᓄᑕᕋᕗᑦ ᐊᑎᖕᒋᑕ ᑐᖅᖢᕋᐅᓯᖕᒋᓐᓂᒃ ᑐᖅᖢᕋᖅᑕᐅᕙᓚᐅᕐᒪᑕ ᑕᐃᑉᓱᒪᓂ. ᐅᑉᓗᒥᐅᓕᖅ ᑐᖅᖢᕋᐅᓰᑦ ᐊᑐᓗᐊᕈᓐᓇᐃᕋᑉᑎᒍ, ᐅᕙᖕᓖᑦᓛᑦ. ᓄᑕᕋᒻᓄᑦ ᐅᖃᖅᐸᒃᑐᖕᒐ, "ᐃᓕᓐᓂᐊᖅᑎᓯᒪᔭᒃᑲ ᐃᓕᑉᓯᓐᓄᑦ ᓄᑕᕋᑉᓯᓐᓄᑦ ᐃᓕᓐᓂᐊᖅᑎᒋᐊᖅᑲᕈᒫᖅᑕᓯ, ᐳᐃᒍᖅᑕᐃᓕᓗᒋᑦ ᐅᖃᐅᓯᕆᕙᓚᐅᖅᑕᒃᑲ ᐃᓕᑉᓯᓐᓄᑦ."

ᐊ. ᑖᓐᓇᓕ ᐊᕝᕙᕆᔭᐅᔪᖅ ᐱᑦᑎᐊᖅᑕᐅᕚᓪᓕᖅᐸᓚᐅᖅᐸ ᐊᐲᐊ ᐱᔾᔪᑕᐅᕝᔪᓃ?

ᑭ. ᐄ, ᐊᑦᑎᖅᓱᓂᖅ ᐱᒻᒪᕆᐅᒻᒪᑦ, ᑖᒻᓇ ᐊᑦᑎᖅᑕᐃᑦ ᖃᓂᒋᔪᖕᓂ ᐱᓗᐊᒃᑲᓂᖅᖢᓂ, ᐊᑦᑎᖅᓯᑦᑕᓕᖅᑎᑦᑐᖕᒐ ᐱᑦᓚᕆᐅᓇᓱᒋᓕᖅᑯᓕ ᐃᓐᓇᕈᖅᐸᓕᐊᑎᑦᑐᖕᒐᓗ. ᐊᑦᑎᖅᓯᑦᑐᓂ ᐅᐱᒋᔭᕐᒥᒃ ᐊᑐᓂᖃᖅᑑᔭᕐᓇᒪᑦ ᐃᓄᐃᑦᑐᓂᓗ. ᐃᖖᒍᑕᕋ ᕉᓯᐅᑉ ᐃᕐᓂᐊ ᐊᑎᓇᒐᑉᑯ, ᑲᖕᒋᖅᓱᓂᕐᒥᐅᑕᐅᒻᒪᑦ ᒫᓇ.

ᐊᐃᕙᓐᒥᒃ ᐊᑎᓕᒃ ᐸᓂᖕᒪ ᐊᑦᑎᕈᐊᓚᐅᕐᒪᒍ ᐅᕙᒻᓂᒃ,ᐊᖏᓚᐅᕋᑉᑯ. ᐊᐃᕙᓐᒥᒃ ᐊᑎᕐᑲᕐᒪᑦ ᐊᖑᑕᐅᒪᑦ ᐊᔪᖏᑦᑑᕐᑯᓚᐅᕋᑉᑯ ᐊᔪᕆᕙᒃᑕᒻᓂᒃ ᐱᔪᖕᓇᕐᓗᓂ, ᐅᕐᑲᕈᓐᓇᑦᑎᐊᕐᓗᓂᓗ ᑐᑭᓯᐊᑦᑎᐊᕐᓗᓂᓗ ᕐᑲᑉᓗᓈᑐᑦ. ᐱᔾᔪᑎᑦᑕᕐᓂᐊᓕᕐᒪᖓ. ᕕᓂᐲᒦᑎᑦᓗᖓ ᐅᕐᑲᓗᓚᐅᕐᒪᑦ ᑮᓯ ᐊᑦᑎᕈᐊᕐᒃᖢᓂᒐ.

ᐊ. ᐅᐱᒋᔭᐅᕚᑦᓕᕐᒃᐲᑦ ᐊᑏᑦ ᐱᔾᔪᑕᐅᑦᓗᓂ ᐃᓚᒋᙱᑕᕋᓗᐊᕐᓄᑦ?

ᑭ. ᐄ ᐅᐱᒋᔭᐅᕚᓕᕐᓇᕐᒃᑐᕐᒃ ᐃᓐᓇᕐᓄᓇᓪᓛ ᑲᖏᕐᒃᓱᓂᕐᒦᑎᑦᓗᖓ ᐅᐱᒋᔭᐅᓚᐅᕐᒪ. ᐅᕐᑲᐅᑎᔭᐅᑦᑕᓚᐅᕐᒪ ᐃᒪᓐᓇ, “ᐊᕝᕙᐃ’ᓂᒻᓇ ᐱᓕᕆᒡᒍᔪᔾᔪᐊᕐᒃ ᐱᓕᕆᐊᕐᒥᓂᒃ ᐱᐊᓂᑦᑎᐊᔪᒻᒫᕐᒃᖢᓂ ᐊᖓᔪᕐᒃᑳᖏᑦᓘᓐᓃᑦ ᑕᒫᓃᖏᑎᑦᓗᒋᑦ.”ᓇᖓᕆᓚᐅᙱᑕᕋ,ᐅᕙᒻᓂᙴᕐᒃ ᐊᔪᖏᓂᕐᒃᓴᐅᒪᑦ. ᕐᑲᑉᓗᓇᐅᔭᑦᑎᐊᕈᓐᓇᕐᒪᑦ ᐱᓕᕆᐊᑦᑎᐊᕐᑲᕐᒃᖢᓂᓗ.

ᐅᑉᓚᓗᓚᐅᕋᑉᑯ ᐊᐃᒐ ᐅᕐᑲᐅᑎᓚᐅᕐᒪᖓ ᐊᕝᕙᑦᑎᐊᕆᖕᓂᕐᒃᖢᖓ. ᐊᐱᕆᓚᐅᕐᒃᑕᕋ ᑭᓇᒥᒃ ᐊᕝᕙᕐᑲᕐᒪᖒᕐᒪ, ᐅᕐᑲᓚᐅᕐᒃᑐᕐᒃ, “ᑭᒪᓕᐊᕐᔪᒃ.” ᐊᐱᕆᓕᕐᒃᖢᒍ “ᓇᓂᕐᒥᐅᑕᕐᒃ?” ᐅᕐᑲᕐᒃᖢᓂ, “ᑕᐃᒻᓇ ᒥᕝᕕᖕᒥ ᐱᓕᕆᔪᕐᒃ.” ᐃᕐᒃᑲᐃᒐᒪ ᐅᕐᑲᓕᕐᒃᖢᖓ ᒥᑖᕐᒃᖢᖓ, “ᓇᖓᕆᙱᑕᕋ ᐅᕙᒻᓂᑦ ᐊᔪᖏᓐᓂᕐᒃᓴᐅᖏᒻᒪᑦ.”

ᐊ. ᓄᑕᕋᕐᒥᒃ ᐊᑦᑎᕐᓂᒃᑐᓂ ᐃᓅᔪᓐᓇᐃᕐᒃᓯᒪᓕᕐᒃᑐᒥᒃ ᑕᒪᓐᓇ ᐃᑲᔪᕚᑦᓕᕈᑕᐅᕙᒃᐸ ᓴᐃᒪᕐᒃᑎᑦᑎᕚᑦᓕᕐᒃᐸᒃᐹ ᑖᒃᑯᓄᖓ ᐃᓚᐃᓚᐅᕐᒃᑐᓄᑦ?

ᑭ. ᐄ ᐃᑲᔪᕐᓂᕐᑲᑦᓚᕆᒃᑐᕐᒃ ᐋᓂᐊᕈᓐᓇᐃᕐᒃᐹᓕᕐᓇᕐᒪᑦ, ᐊᒻᒪ ᒪᒥᑉᐹᑦᓕᕐᓇᕐᒃᖢᓂ. ᐃᓚᒋᔭᐃᑦ ᐊᖓᔪᕐᒃᑳᓘᓐᓃᑦ ᐊᑎᕐᒃᑕᐅᔭᖔᕐᒐᑦ ᐃᓚᒋᙱᑕᕋᓗᐊᕐᒧᑦ ᒪᒥᑉᐹᓕᕐᓇᑐᕐᒃ. ᕐᑯᔭᓕᓚᕆᒃᑐᖓ ᐊᓅᓇᒐ ᐊᑦᑎᕐᒃᑕᐅᓚᐅᕐᒪᑦ ᑲᖏᕐᒃᓱᓂᕐᒥ ᐊᕐᓇᕐᑲᑎᖏᓐᓄᑦ ᑖᕙᓂᒥᐅᑕᓄᑦ.

ᐃᓱᒪᒃᑯᑦ ᓴᐃᒻᒪᕐᒃᐹᑦᓕᑦᑎᐊᓚᐅᕐᒪ

ᐃᓱᒪᑦᑎᐊᕐᓂᖅᓴᐅᔫᔭᓕᖅᑕᖓᑕ. ᐅᓚᐱᖅᓴᐅᑎᑖᒃᑲᓐᓂᖅᑕᖓ ᖁᔭᓕᑦᑎᐊᓕᖅᑕᖓᑕ ᐊᑦᑎᖅᑕᐅᒻᒪᑦ ᐋᓈᓇ. ᐅᕙᒻᒥᑦᓖᓛᒃ ᐊᑦᑎᖅᓯᓂᖅ ᐱᒻᒪᕆᐅᒻᒪᑦ ᐱᖅᑯᓯᕆᒐᑉᑎᒍ ᑲᔪᓯᔭᕆᐊᖃᕐᒪᑦ ᐊᑑᑎᖃᒻᒪᕆᖕᒪᑦ.

ᐊ. ᐅᑉᓗᒥᐅᓕᖅᑐᕐᓕ ᑐᖅᓱᕋᐅᓰᑦ ᐊᔾᔭᐅᓕᖅᐸᑦ?

ᑭ. ᐄ, ᐊᔾᔭᐅᑦᓚᓇᓕᖅᑐᖅ ᑕᐃᑉᓯᒪᓂ ᐃᓚᓗᒃᑖᑉᑎᓐᓂᒃ ᑐᖅᓱᕋᖅᐸᓚᐅᕋᓗᐊᕋᑉᑕ. ᐊᑖᑕᒐᓗ ᓄᑲᙶᓗ ᓄᑕᕋᑐᐊᖑᓚᐅᕐᒪᓂᒃ ᐊᒻᒪ ᓄᑕᕋᕐᑲᐅᖅᓱᑎᒍᑦ. ᐊᑖᑕᒪ ᓄᑲᙵ ᒪᑦᖀᓐᓂᒃ ᐃᕐᓂᕐᑲᕐᒪᑦ ᒪᑦᖀᓐᓂᒡᓗ ᐸᓂᕐᑲᖅᓱᓂ. ᐊᕐᓇᐅᔪᒃ ᑖᒃᑯᐊᒃ ᐊᖑᑎᕐᑲᑎᕆᒐᑉᑭᒃ ᐊᒻᒪ ᐃᕐᓂᖕᕆᒃ ᑕᒪᕐᒥᒃ ᐃᓅᔪᓐᓇᐃᖅᓯᒪᔪᒃ ᐊᓂᒃᓴᓇᓚᐅᖅᓱᕆᒃ ᐊᒃᑲᖕᒪ ᓄᑕᕋᓇᖕᒪᕆᒃ.

ᐊᓂᒐ ᐃᓅᓴᖅ, ᑐᖅᓱᕋᖅᑕᕋ ᐊᓂᑯᓗᒻᓂᒃ ᐊᒻᒪ ᐊᖕᒐᖕᒪ ᐃᕐᓂᕆᑦ ᑕᐃᒪᓐᓇᒃᓴᐃᓐᓇᖅ ᑐᖅᓱᕋᐅᓯᖅ ᐊᓂᑯᓗᒃ ᐊᑐᓇᑉᓗᒍ. ᐊᑐᑦᓚᓇᒃᐸᓚᐅᕋᑉᑕ ᑐᖅᓱᕋᖅᑐᕋᐅᑦᓗᓇᒃᓴᑎᐊᖅᓱᑕ.

ᐊ. ᖃᓄᕐᓕ ᐊᑦᑎᖅᑐᐃᓂᖅ ᐃᓄᒃᑐᑦ ᐊᑐᖅᑎᒋᕙ?

ᑭ. ᐃᓕᑦᑎᓚᐅᕋᒪ ᐊᓈᓇᑦᑎᐊᒻᓂᑦ. ᐅᖃᐅᔾᔪᖅᐸᓚᐅᕐᒪᙶ ᐊᒥᓱᓂᒃ ᐃᓅᓯᕐᒧᑦ ᑐᕌᖅᑐᓂᒃ ᓯᕗᓂᕐᒧᑦ. ᐅᓇᑉᑕᐅᖅ ᐅᖃᐅᓯᓇᕙᓚᐅᖅᑖ ᓯᕗᓂᕐᒧᑦ ᐸᕐᓇᒃᓯᒪᔭᓇᐊᕐᑲᕐᓂᖅ ᓱᓗᕐᑭᒋᐊᓚᐅᖅᑳᕋᓂ. ᐊᑦᑎᖅᑐᐃᓂᖅ ᐱᒻᒪᕆᐅᒻᒪᑦ ᐅᔾᔨᕆᔭᐅᑦᑎᐊᕆᐊᖃᕐᒪᑦ, ᐃᓐᓇᕆᔭᐅᔪᓂᑦ ᐊᐱᕆᖅᑳᕐᓗᑎᒃ ᑭᓱᐊᓂ ᐱᔭᕆᐊᖃᕐᒪᑕ ᐊᑦᑎᖅᓯᔪᒪᔪᑦ. ᒪᓕᒐᖅᑲᖅᐸᓚᐅᕐᒪᑕ ᓯᕗᓕᕗᑦ. ᐊᑦᑎᖅᑐᐃᕙᓕᓚᐅᕐᒪ ᓄᑕᕋᓂᒃ ᐊᖓᔪᒃᖠᖅᐸᙱᓕᕐᒪ ᐃᓚᓗᒃᑖᑉᑎᓐᓂᒃ. ᐊᓂᒐ ᐹ ᓄᑲᖅᖠᐸᙱᑉᓗᓂ. ᐱᖓᓱᓐᓃᖔᓕᕋᑦ: ᐅᕙᖓᓗ, ᓯᔫᓇᓗ ᐹᓗ.

ᐸᓂᖓ ᖀᓯᐅᑉ ᐊᐱᓈᓇᔭᖕᒪᖓ ᐊᑦᑎᖅᓯᔭᕆᐊᖃᓕᖔᖓᒥ

ᓄᑕᕋᖅᑖᕌᖓᒥᒃ. ᐅᖃᐅᑎᓚᐅᖅᓯᒪᔭᕋ ᐃᓅᓯᑉᑎᓐᓂ ᐊᒥᓯᔪᐃᑦ ᐊᓪᓚᕈᓯᒪᓕᕐᒪᓪ.

ᒪᒃᑯᒃᑐᑦ ᐃᓚᖏᑦ ᖃᐅᔨᑎᑦᑎᑦᑕᖏᒪᑕ ᐊᖑᔪᖅᑳᒥᓐᓂᒃ ᓄᑕᕋᖅᑖᕋᓗᐊᕌᖓᒥᒃ, ᐊᒥᓯᐃᖅᖁᑎᒃ ᐊᑖᑕᑦᑎᐊᖏᓪᓗ ᐊᓈᓇᑦᑎᐊᖏᓪᓗ ᓄᑕᕋᖅᑖᕋᓗᐊᕌᖓᑕ ᖃᐅᔨᒪᕙᖏᒻᒪᑕ ᓱᓇᑖᕐᒪᖔᑦ. ᑕᒪᓐᓇ ᓈᒪᖏᑦᑕᓇᒃᑐᖅ ᑭᓯᐊᓂ ᖃᓄᖅ ᐱᓂᖅ ᓇᓗᓇᖅᑐᖅ. ᐊᑦᑎᖅᑐᐃᓂᖅ ᐱᒻᒪᕆᐅᒪᑦ ᐅᑉᓗᒥᒧᑦ ᐃᓕᖅᑯᓯᕗᑦ ᐊᑐᕆᐊᖃᕋᑉᑎᒍ. ᐃᓅᕐᒥᒃ ᐊᑦᑎᖅᓯᔪᒪᒍᑉᑕ ᐃᒻᒪᖄ ᓴᑭᒋᔭᐅᔪᒥᒃ ᐊᐱᕆᐸᓈᐸᒃᑐᒍᑦ ᓱᓕ. ᐃᓐᓇᕆᔭᐅᔪᑦ ᐊᑦᑎᓯᔭᕆᐊᖃᔪᖕᒪᑕ. ᑕᐃᒪᓐᓇᐃᖏᓐᓇᖅᐸᓚᐅᕐᒪᑦ ᑕᐃᒪᓐᓇᐃᒋᐊᖃᖅᐳᖅ ᓱᓕ ᐊᑦᑎᖅᓯᓂᐊᕐᓗᓂ.

ᐊ. ᑕᐃᑉᓱᒪᓂᓕ ᐊᑦᑎᖅᑐᐃᓂᕐᓗ ᑐᖅᖁᕋᕐᓂᕐᓗ ᐊᑐᖅᑕᐅᑎᐊᓚᐅᖅᐸ?

ᑭ. ᐄᓪᓚᕆᒃ, ᑐᖅᖁᕋᖅᑐᕋᐅᓪᓗᕆᒃᓴᖅᐸᓚᐅᕋᑉᑕ ᐃᓚᓗᒃᑖᑦᑎᓐᓂᒃ ᐊᑐᖅᑕᐅᑦᑎᐊᓚᐅᖅᑐᖅ. ᐅᕙᖔᓪᓛᑦ ᐊᑐᐃᓇᖅᐸᓚᐅᕋᑉᑯ ᐃᓚᓗᒃᑖᒻᓄᑦ ᑕᐃᑉᓱᒪᓂ. ᖃᐅᔨᑐᐊᕌᖓᑉᑕ ᐃᓚᒌᖕᓂᑉᑎᓐᓂᒃ ᑐᖅᖁᕋᓕᑲᐅᑎᒋᕙᓚᐅᕋᑉᑎᒍ ᐊᑦᑖᓛᕐᓗᒋᓪᓘᕝᕙ ᐊᖔᓚᕐᓗᒋᓪᓘᕝᕙ. ᐅᑉᓗᒥᐅᓕᖅᑐᖅ ᐃᓐᓇᓄᓇᒡᓛᑦ ᓱᕐᑯᑕᐅᖏᓕᕐᒪᑦ ᐊᓯᐅᔨᓯᒪᓗᐊᓕᕋᑉᑕ ᐅᖃᐅᓯᑉᑎᓐᓂᒃ. ᐅᑉᓗᒥᐅᓕᖅᑐᖅ ᒪᒃᑯᒃᑐᑦ ᑲᑉᓗᓈᑐᐃᓐᓇᖅ ᐅᖃᖅᑕᓕᕐᒪᑕ.

ᐊ. ᑐᖅᖁᕋᕐᓂᖅ ᐊᔾᔨᒌᖏᑉ ᐃᓄᖕᓄᑦ ᐃᓚᒌᖏᑐᓄᑦ?

ᑭ. ᐄ ᑕᐃᒪᓐᓇᐃᑐᖅ ᐅᕙᑉᑎᓐᓄᑦ. ᑕᒫᓂ ᑭᕙᓪᓕᕐᒥᐅᑕᐅᖏᓐᓇᕋᒪ. ᐊᓈᓇᒐ ᐊᕐᕕᐊᕐᒥᐅᑕᐅᒻᒪᑦ ᐊᑖᑕᒐ ᐅᒃᑯᓯᒃᓴᓕᖕᒥᐅᑕᐅᑉᓗᓂ ᑕᒃᐹᓂᖅᐸᓯᒃ. ᐊᑖᑕᒐ ᐊᓈᓇᑦᑎᐊᒻᓃᒥᓐᓇᓚᐅᕐᒪᑦ ᐊᕐᓇᕐᑯᐊᓵᖑᑎᐊᖅᖁᓂ. ᐊᓈᓇᑦᑎᐊᕐᒪ ᐃᓕᓐᓂᐊᖅᑎᓯᒪᕐᔪᐊᕐᒪᑎᒍᑦ

ᑐᖅᓱᕋᐅᓯᕐᓂᒃ, ᐅᐃᖅᑲᕐᓂᒥᒃ, ᓄᑕᖅᑭᐅᕐᓂᕐᒥᒃ ᐊᒻᒪ ᒥᖅᓱᕐᓂᕐᒥᒃ ᐅᑭᐅᖅᓯᐅᑎᓂᒃ ᐊᐅᔭᖅᓯᐅᑎᓂᒡᓗ. ᐊᒥᓱᕐᔪᐊᕐᓂᒃ ᐊᔪᕐᑭᖅᑐᖅᓯᒪᖕᒪᑎᒍᑦ.

ᑕᐃᒪᖕᒐᓂᑦ ᓄᓇᓕᖕᒥᐅᑕᐅᓕᕋᑉᑕ ᐃᒡᓗᔪᐊᕐᒥᐅᑕᐅᓕᖅᓱᑕᓗ, ᐃᓕᓐᓂᐊᖅᑎᑎᔪᓐᓇᐃᑦᓕᒐᑉᑕ ᐃᓕᓐᓂᐊᖅᑎᑕᐅᓂᑯᑉᑎᓐᓂᒃ. ᐃᓐᓇᐃᓇᒡᒑᑦ ᖃᐅᔨᒪᑦᑎᐊᖅᑐᑦ ᐃᓕᓐᓂᐊᖅᑎᑕᐅᑦᑎᐊᕐᓂᑯᑦ ᐊᒥᖅᑳᖅᑲᑎᖅᑲᖅᑕᖕᒋᖕᒪᑕ ᐃᓕᓐᓂᐊᖅᑎᑦᑎᖕᒋᔅᓱᑎᒡᓗ ᓄᑕᕋᑉᑎᓐᓂᒃ. ᐊᓯᔾᔨᕐᔪᐊᖅᓯᒪᔪᔾᔫᒐᑉᑕ ᐃᓅᒃᑎᒍᑦ ᐱᖅᑯᓯᑉᑎᒍᑦ ᐃᓅᓯᑉᑎᓐᓂᓗ ᐊᔪᓇᕈᑕᐅᕐᔪᐊᓕᕐᒪᑦ ᑕᒪᓐᓇ. ᐱᐅᓂᖅᑲᖅᑑᒐᓗᐊᖅ ᑭᓯᐊᓂ ᐊᔪᓇᕈᑎᖃᖅᑐᖅ ᐊᒥᓱᓂᒃ ᐃᓐᓇᐅᓂᖅᓴᓄᑦ.

ᓈᓐᓯ ᑕᔅᓯᐅᖅ

ᐊᐱᖅᓱᖅᑕᐅᒪᑦ ᐅᑉᓗᐊ
ᐊᑯᓪᓚᕈᕐᕕᒃ 2012

ᐊ. ᐅᖃᐅᑎᔫᓪᓗᐊᖅᐱᖓ ᖃᓄᖅ ᐊᑦᑎᖅᑐᐃᓱᕐᒪᖔᑖ?

ᑭ. ᐃᓚᒃᑲ ᐅᑯᐊᖑᒪᑕ, ᐸᓂᒃᑲ, ᐃᕐᓂᒃᑲ, ᓴᑮᒃᑲᓗ. ᑐᖅᖢᕋᖅᐸᒃᑲᑉᑯ ᓄᑕᕋᕋ ᐊᑖᑕᒻᓂ ᐊᑎᖃᖅᐸᑦ ᐊᑦᑎᐊᒻᓂᒃ. ᑎᐊ'ᐊ ᐊᖓᔪᖅᑳᕐᒪ ᐊᔪᕿᖅᑐᓯᒪᖕᒪᖓ ᐊᑐᖅᐸᒃᑲᑉᑭᑦ ᐃᓕᑦᑎᓐᓂᑯᒃᑲ ᐊᖓᔪᖅᑳᒻᓂᑦ. ᐃᓚᒌᑎᒍᑦ ᑐᖅᖢᕋᖅᑐᕋᐅᓯᕋᑉᑕ ᐊᑏᓂᒃ ᐊᑐᖏᔅᖢᑕ. ᐃᓚᖏᑦ ᐃᓚᒌᑦ ᓄᑕᕋᖅ ᐊᑖᑖᓂᒃ ᐊᑎᖃᖅᐸᑦ ᐊᑖᑖᓛᓱᕐᒪᑕ ᐅᕙᓘᓃᑦ ᐊᓈᓈᓂᒃ ᐊᑎᖃᖅᐸᑦ ᐊᓈᓈᓛᖅᖢᒍ. ᑎᐊ'ᐊᐃᒪᑦ ᐅᑉᓗᒥ. ᓄᑲᕋᓘᕝᕙ ᐊᖓᔪᒐᓘᕝᕙ ᐊᕐᓇᖃᑎᒐᓘᕝᕙ ᐅᐃᑖᖅᐸᑦ ᐊᐃᑖᖅᐸᒃᑐᒍᑦ ᐊᒻᒪ ᐊᐃᒋᔅᐅᓕᖅᖢᑕ ᑕᐃᑯᖓ ᐅᐃᑖᓇᔾᔭᓄᑦ. ᐊᑏᓂᒃ ᐊᑐᖅᑕᖏᑦᑐᒍᑦ ᑲᖕᖑᓇᕐᒪᑦ ᐊᐃᑎᓐᓂᒃ ᐊᖑᖅᑐᕋᐃᔪᓂ, ᐅᖃᖃᑎᒋᔭᓇᐊᖃᖏᑕᕗᑦᓘᓐᓃᑦ ᑕᒪᓐᓇ ᐱᖅᑯᓯᐅᒪᑦ ᐅᐱᒋᑐᕐᐅᓗᐊᒧᑦ.

ᐊ. ᓄᑕᕋᒥᒡᓕ ᐊᑦᑎᖅᓯᒍᕕᑦ ᑖᒻᓇ ᐊᕝᕚᑕ ᑐᖅᖢᕋᐅᓯᐊᓂᒃ ᐊᑐᕐᓗᓂ ᑐᖅᖢᕋᖅᑕᐅᓇᔭᖅᐸ?

ᑭ. ᐊᑎᓖᑦ ᐅᕙᑉᑎᓂᒃ ᐊᕝᕙᓖᔪᔭᕗᑦ. ᐃᓄᐃᑦ ᐅᖃᐅᓯᐊᑦ ᐊᑐᕐᓗᒍ ᐊᕝᕙᕇᒃ, ᑐᑭᓕᒃ ᐃᓅᒃ ᐊᔾᔨᒌᓂᒃ ᐊᑎᓖᒃ. ᓄᑕᕋᕗᑦ ᐃᓐᓇᑉᑎᓐᓂᒃ ᐊᑦᑎᖅᓯᒪᔪᑦ, ᐅᕙᖕᖔᓛᑦ ᐊᑎᖃᕋᒪ ᐊᕝᕚᓖᔪᔭᒃᑲ, ᐊᒥᓱᔾᔪᐊᕐᓂᒃ ᓇᓂᓗᒃᑖᖅ ᐊᕝᕙᖃᕋᒪ. ᐅᕙᑉᑎᑐᑦ ᐊᑦᑎᖅᑕᐅᓯᒪᔭᕚᖓᑕ ᐊᕝᕚᓖᓯᕋᑉᑎᒍ.

ᐊ. ᓄᑕᕋᕐᒥᒃ ᐊᑦᑎᕐᓂᒃᑯᓂ ᐃᓅᔪᓐᓇᐃᖅᓯᒪᓕᖅᑯᒥᒃ ᑕᒪᓐᓇ ᐃᑲᔪᕚᑦᓕᕈᑕᐅᕙᒃᐹ ᓴᐃᒪᖅᑎᑦᑎᕚᑦᓕᖅᐸᒃᐹ ᑳᒃᑯᓄᖓ ᐃᓚᐃᓚᐅᖅᑯᓄᑦ?

ᑭ. ᐄ, ᐊᑦᑎᕐᓂᖕᓂᐊᕐᓗᓂ ᐃᓅᔪᓐᓇᐃᖅᓯᒪᓕᖅᑯᒥᒃ ᐅᑕᖅᑭᓚᐅᕆᐊᕐᑲᓱᖅᑯᑦ. ᐃᓅᔪᓐᓇᐃᖅᓯᒪᓕᖅᑯᑦ ᐊᑦᑎᖅᑕᐅᔭᕌᖓᑕ ᐄ ᓴᐃᒪᐹᑦᓕᕐᓇᖅᑯᖅ, ᐃᓱᒪᒃᑯᑦᓗ ᐊᒃᓱᕈᓗᐊᕈᓐᓇᐃᓇᖅᓱᓂ. ᓄᑕᕋᓛᖕᒍᒐᓗᐊᕈᒥᓘᓐᓃᑦ ᓈᒻᒪᒃᑯᖅ ᐃᓅᔪᓐᓇᐃᖅᓯᒪᓕᖅᑯᖅ ᐊᑦᑎᖅᑕᐅᔭᕌᖓᑦ ᐃᓕᑦᑎᐊᕚᓕᕐᓇᑦᓗᐊᖏᒃᑯᖅ.

ᐊ. ᐅᐸᓗᒥᐅᓕᖅᑯᕐᓕ ᑐᖅᓱᕋᐅᓰᑦ ᐊᔾᔨᐅᓕᖅᐸᑦ?

ᑭ. ᐄ, ᑐᓴᖅᑕᓕᕋᒪ ᑐᖅᓱᕋᐅᓯᕐᓂᒃ ᐊᑐᖅᐸᓚᐅᖕᒋᑕᑉᑎᓂᒃ ᐃᒻᒪᖄ ᓄᓇᓕᖕᓂᑦ ᐊᓯᖕᒋᓂᑦ ᐊᔪᕐᑲᖅᑭᕙᓪᓕᐊᓕᕐᒪᑕ. ᑳᒃᑯᐊ ᑐᓴᕋᔪᙱᓚᐅᒃᑲᕗᑦ ᐅᐸᓗᒥᐅᓕᖅ ᐊᑐᖅᑕᐅᕙᓕᕐᒪᑕ. ᐅᓇᑉᑕᐅᖅ ᐃᓯᓖᓗᒋᕙᒃᑕᕋ ᐊᑏᓂᒃ ᓇᐃᑦᑐᓈᓂᒃ ᑐᖅᓱᕋᔪᓯᒻᒪᑕ. ᐆᒃᑐᑎᒋᓗᒍ ᖃᐅᓐᓇᖅ ᓇᐃᓈᕐᓗᒍ ᖃᐅᓐ. ᐃᒻᒪᖄ ᐊᒃᑐᑦ ᒪᒃᑯᑐᒥ'ᓂᒃ ᐊᔪᕐᑲᖅᑭᒥᐊᓕᕐᒪᑕ.

ᐊ. ᖃᓄᕐᓕ ᐊᑦᑎᕐᓂᖕᓂᖅ ᓄᑕᕋᕐᒥᒃ ᐊᑐᖅᑎᒋᕙ?

ᑭ. ᖃᖕᒑ'ᓈᖅ ᐃᓄᐃᑦ ᐃᓄᒃᑐᐃᓐᓇᖅ ᐊᑏᓂᒃ ᐊᑐᔪᓚᐅᕋᓗᐊᕐᒪᑕ ᖃᑉᓗᓈᑐᐃᓐᓇᖅ ᐊᑐᐸᑦᓕᐊᓕᓚᐅᖅᑰᑦ ᐊᔪᕐᑭᖅᑐᐃᔨᑦ ᑯᕝᕕᕆᓂᒃᑕᓕᕐᒪᑕ. ᐃᓚᖕᒋᓯᓕ ᐃᓄᒃᑯᑦ ᐊᑏᓂᒃ ᐊᑐᔪᔫᒐᓗᐃᑦ ᖃᐅᔨᒪᖕᒋᓕᒃᑲᒃᑲᔫᓂᑦ.

ᐊ. ᑕᐃᑉᓯᒪᓂᓕ ᐊᑦᑎᖅᑐᐃᓂᕐᓗ ᑐᖅᓱᕋᕐᓂᕐᓗ ᐊᑐᖅᑕᐅᑎᐊᓚᐅᖅᐸ?

ᑭ. ᐄᓚᐅᖑᒐᓗᐊᖅ. ᑕᐃᑉᓱᒪᓂ ᐃᓄᒃᑐᐃᓐᓇᖅ ᐅᖃᒻᒫᔪᓚᐅᕋᑉᑕ ᑐᖅᖢᕋᐅᓯᖅ ᐊᑐᑦᓗᓇᒃᓴᓚᐅᖅᑐᖅ. ᐃᓚᒌᓂᕗᑦᓗ ᐱᒡᒍᓂᖅᓴᐅᑉᓗᓂ ᐃᓚᒌᓗᒃᑳᖅᑑᓴᔪᓚᐅᕋᑉᑕ. ᐅᑉᓗᒥᐅᓕᖅ ᑭᑐᓂᒃ ᐃᓚᖃᕐᒪᖕᒑᑉᑕ ᖃᐅᔨᒪᓐᓇᖏᒥᐊᓕᖅᑐᖅ ᑐᖅᖢᕋᖅᑐᕋᐅᔪᓐᓇᐃᒥᐊᕋᑉᑕ.

ᐊ. ᑕᐃᑉᓱᒪᓂᓕ ᐊᑦᑎᖅᑐᐃᓂᕐᓗ ᑐᖅᖢᕋᕐᓂᕐᓗ ᐊᑐᖅᑕᐅᑎᐊᓚᐅᖅᐸ?

ᑭ. ᐄᓚᐅᖑᒐᓗᐊᖅ. ᑕᐃᑉᓱᒪᓂ ᐃᓄᒃᑐᐃᓐᓇᖅ ᐅᖃᒻᒫᔪᓚᐅᕋᑉᑕ ᑐᖅᖢᕋᐅᓯᖅ ᐊᑐᑦᓗᓇᒃᓴᓚᐅᖅᑐᖅ. ᐃᓚᒌᓂᕗᑦᓗ ᐱᒡᒍᓂᖅᓴᐅᑉᓗᓂ ᐃᓚᒌᓗᒃᑳᖅᑑᓴᔪᓚᐅᕋᑉᑕ. ᐅᑉᓗᒥᐅᓕᖅ ᑭᑐᓂᒃ ᐃᓚᖃᕐᒪᖕᒑᑉᑕ ᖃᐅᔨᒪᓐᓇᖏᒥᐊᓕᖅᑐᖅ ᑐᖅᖢᕋᖅᑐᕋᐅᔪᓐᓇᐃᒥᐊᕋᑉᑕ.

ᐊ. ᑐᖅᖢᕋᕐᓂᖅ ᐊᔾᔨᒌᖏᐸ ᐃᓄᖕᓄᑦ ᐃᓚᒌᖏᑐᓄᑦ?

ᑭ. ᐄ ᑐᓴᕋᔪᐃᕐᑐᔾᔫᒐᒪ ᑐᖅᖢᕋᖅᑐᕋᐅᕐᑐᓂᒃ ᐃᓚᖏᓂᒃ ᑐᑭᓯᕙᖏᑐᖓ. ᓯᕗᓪᓕᖅᐹᒥᒃ ᑐᓴᕋᒪ ᑐᖅᖢᕋᐅᓯᕐᒥᒃ ᑕᒫᓂᕐᒥᐅᑕᐅᖏᑦᑐᒥᒃ ᑐᑭᓯᓚᐅᖏᑐᖓ. ᑐᓵᕌᖕᒐᒪᓘᓐᓃᑦ ᑐᑭᓯᕙᖏᑐᖓᓯᓕ. ᐊᕐᕕᐊᓂᓕ ᑐᖅᖢᕋᖅᑐᕋᐅᓯᕐᒪᑕ. ᐊᕐᓇᖅᑲᑎᒌᑦ ᐃᓚᓐᓈᓅᑦᓘᓐᓃᑦ ᐃᓄᒃᑐᑦ ᐊᑏᓂᒃ ᐊᑐᔪᒻᒪᑕ.

ᑐᖅ ᖢᖁᐅᓰᑦ

ᑐᖅᓕᐊ
ᐊᑑᑎᖕᒋᑦ ᐊᒻᒪ
ᐱᒻᒪᕆᐅᓂᖕᒋᑦ ᑐᖢᖁᐅᓰᑦ

ᓕᐅ ᐃᓐᓇᐅᓂᖁᓴᖅ ᐋᒻᒪᖅ
ᐊᐱᖅᓱᖅᑕᐅᒪᑦ ᐅᐸᓗᐊ
ᓴᒡᒋᕆᕝᕕᒃ 2012

ᐊ. ᑐᓴᐅᒪᒐᑉᑯ ᓴᐅᓂᕇᒃ. ᖃᓄᖅ ᑖᒻᓇ ᐊᑐᖅᑕᐅᓇᔭᖅᐸ?

ᑭ. ᐄ, ᑐᓴᐅᒪᔭᕋ ᓴᐅᓂᕇᑦ ᐊᒻᒪ ᐊᒪᐅᖅ. ᐃᓄᒻᒪᕆᐅᒐᒪ ᑕᒪᒃᑯᐊ

ᖃᐅᔨᒪᔭᒃᑲ ᓯᕗᓕᕆᓚᐅᖅᑕᑉᑕ ᐊᑐᔪᓚᐅᒐᐃ. ᓴᐅᓂᖅ ᐃᙳᑕᕐᒪ ᓄᑕᕋᕆᖕᒪᒍ ᐊᒻᒪ ᐊᒪᐅᑖᕋᔭᕐᒪᖓ.

ᐊ. ᑐᖅᓱᕋᓂᖅ ᐊᕐᓇᓄᑦᑐ ᐊᖑᑎᓄᑦᑐ ᐊᔾᔨᒌᖏᑉᐸ?

ᑭ. ᐄ, ᐊᔾᔨᒌᖏᑦᑐᖅ. ᐊᖑᑎᑦᑐ ᐊᕐᓇᐃᑦᑐ ᑐᖅᓱᕋᐅᓯᖃᐅᕐᒪᑕ. ᐊᔾᔨᒌᖏᓐᓂᑦᑕᓕᕐᔪᐊᖅ ᐊᒻᒪ ᑐᑭᖃᑦᑎᐊᖅᓱᑎᒃ.

ᐊ. ᑭᑐᓂᒃ ᐊᑎᖃᖅᐱᑦ ᐊᒻᒪ ᖃᑉᐱᓂᒃ ᐊᑎᖃᖅᐱᑦ?

ᑭ. ᐊᑎᖃᖅᑐᖓ ᐋᒻᒪᖅ, ᐃᓅᓴᖅᑎᑦᑐᖓ ᐅᕙᒻᓄᑦ ᑐᓂᔭᐅᓚᐅᖅᑐᖅ, ᑕᐃᒪᙵᓂᑦ ᐊᑎᕆᔭᕋ. ᐊᒻᒪᓗ ᓕᐅᒥᒃ ᐃᒃᓯᕋᔪᐊᕐᓄᑦ ᐊᑦᑎᖅᑕᐅᓕᕆᑉᓗᖓ, ᐊᒻᒪ ᐊᓯᐊᕐᒥᐅᑦ ᑎᑭᖃᕐᒪᑕ ᑕᒪᐅᖓ ᖄᕐᔭᐅ ᓇᒡᓕᒋᖂᖅᓱᓂᖓ ᐊᐱᕆᖕᒪᖓ, “ᑭᓇᐅᕕᑦ?” ᑭᐅᒐᒃᑯ, “ᐋᒻᒪᖅ.” ᐅᖃᖅᓱᓂ, “ᐄ-ᐄ ᐋᒻᒪᓈᖅ,” ᑕᐃᒪᙵᓂᑦ ᐋᒻᒪᓈᖑᓕᖅᓱᖓ.

ᐊ. ᑐᓴᐅᒪᔭᖃᖅᐱᑦ ᐊᑎᖅᑖᕈᐊᖏᑦᑐᒥᒃ ᐅᕝᕙᓘᕝᕙ ᐊᑎᖅᑖᕈᐊᖅᑐᒥᒃ ᐃᓚᒋᙱᑕᕋᓗᐊᒥᓂᒃ?

ᑭ. ᓄᑕᕋᕐᓂᒃ ᐊᑦᑎᓂᒍᐊᓕᕈᕕᑦ ᐃᓚᒋᖏᑕᕐᓂᒃ ᐊᐱᕆᔭᕆᐊᖃᕈᒫᖅᑐᑎᑦ ᐃᓐᓇᕆᔭᐃᓄᑦ ᓈᒪᒃᑲᓗᐊᕐᒪᖔᑦ. ᑎᐊ'ᐊ ᐱᖅᑯᓯᐅᒪᑦ ᐃᓐᓇᖅ ᐊᑎᖅᑖᕈᐊᓕᕈᒥ ᐊᐱᕆᕙᒌᓯᕐᒪᑕ.

ᐊ. ᑐᓴᐅᒪᔭᖃᖏᑉᐱᓪᓕ ᐊᑎᒃᓴᖃᖏᑦᑐᒥᒃ ᐃᓅᓴᖅᑐᒥᒃ ᓄᑕᕋᕖᒥᒃ?

ᑭ. ᖃᐅᔨᒪᔪᖓ ᒪᒃᑯᒃᑐᖅ ᐊᕐᓇᖅ ᓄᑕᕋᖅᑖᖅᐸᑦ ᖃᑉᓗᓈᑐᑦ ᐊᑦᑎᓯᒪᔾᔪᒃ

ᐊᒻᒪ ᐊᖓᔪᖅᑳᖕᒋᑕ ᐃᓄᒃᑐᑦ ᐊᑦᑎᖅᓱᓂᔾᔪᒃ. ᐃᒻᒪᖅᑳ ᐃᓚᒥᓐᓂᒃ ᖃᐅᔨᒪᑦᑎᐊᖕᒋᓇᒥᒃ ᐃᓄᐃᑦᑐ ᐱᖅᑯᓯᑐᖅᑲᓇᖕᒪᔾᔪᒃ ᐊᑦᑎᖅᑐᐃᓂᖅ.

ᐊ. ᖃᐅᔨᒪᔾᖅᑲᖕᒋᑉᐱᑦᑕ ᐊᑎᖅᑳᑕᖅᑐᒥ ᐃᓅᓚᐅᖅᑳᖅᑎᓐᓇᒍ ᓄᑕᕌᖅ?

ᑭ. ᐃᓄᐃᑦ ᐃᓚᖕᒋᑦ ᐊᑎᕐᓂᒃ ᐃᓯᒪᓯᒫᑕᔪᒻᒪᑕ ᓄᑕᕌᖅ ᐃᓅᓚᐅᖅᑳᑎᓐᓇᒍᐊᑖᖅ. ᐃᑖᓐᓂᒃᑯᑦ ᓯᓐᓇᒃᑑᒪᐃᓐᓇᓕᖅᑳᖓᒥᒃ ᐃᓅᖖᒋᓕᖅᑐᒥᒃ ᑕᒪᓐᓇ ᑐᑭᖅᑲᔪᒻᒪ ᐊᑦᑎᖅᑕᐅᓯᐊᖅᒪᑦ.

ᐊ. ᓄᑕᕋᐅᑎᔾᔪᑎᑦ ᐱᕈᖅᑲᑎᔾᔪᑎᑦ ᐃᓕᓐᓂᐊᖅᑎᑕᐅᓚᐅᖅᐱᑦ ᐊᑎᕐᓂᒃ?

ᑭ. ᐊᑎᒻᓂ ᐃᓕᓐᓂᐊᖅᑎᑕᐅᖕᒋᑕᐃᓇᖅᑐᖕᒐ ᑭᓯᐊᓂ ᖃᐅᔨᒪᓚᐅᖅᑐᖕᒐ ᐊᑖᑦᑕᖃᔪᑉᑎᓂᒃ ᐃᓚᑦᑎᓂᓪᓗ ᐊᑦᑎᖅᑕᐅᓯᖃᑉᑕ. ᐊᓈᓇᒪ ᐊᑦᑎᓚᐅᕐᓂᕐᒪᖕᒐ ᐊᐃᒥᓂᒃ ᐋᒻᒪᕐᒥᒃ. ᑖᒻᓇ ᐊᑎᖅ ᐊᓈᓇᒪ ᖃᐃᓚᐅᖅᑖ ᐅᕙᑉᑎᖕᓂ ᐃᓚᑉᑎᓅᖕᒋᓇᖅᑐᖅ.

ᐊ. ᖃᐅᔨᓯᒪᕕᑦ ᑭᓇᒥᐊᒥᒃ ᐊᑎᓇᔪᕐᒥᓂᒃ ᐃᑲᔪᖅᑕᐅᔪᒥᒃ?

ᑭ. ᐃᓄᐃᑦ ᐃᓐᓇᐃ ᐃᓚᖕᒋᑦ ᐅᖅᑲᔪᖕᒪᑕ ᑐᑭᓯᐊᑉᓗᑎᒡᓗ ᓇᒡᓕᒍᓯᑦᓗᐊᕝᑯᑉᑕᒎᖅ ᓄᑕᕋᑉᑎᓐᓂᒃ ᐃᓕᓐᓂᐊᖅᑎᒋᐊᖅᑲᕋᑉᑎᒍ ᐱᓕᕆᔪᓴᕐᓗᒋᑦ ᐱᕈᖅᐸᓪᓕᐊᑎᔾᔪᒋᑦ. ᓈᒻᒪᖕᓂᖅᓴᐅᒪᑦ ᐱᓕᕆᑎᑕᐅᑦᑕᖅᑐᓂ ᓯᓕᕆᐊᒃᓴᓂᒃ ᕿᓂᔪᖕᒪᑕ ᐱᑦᑎᐊᕈᓇᐃᓕᖅᓱᑎᒡᓗ ᓯᑦᓗᐊᖕᒋᓕᖀᖕᒐᒥᒃ. ᐊᕝᕙᐃᑦ ᐊᔪᙱᕐᑯᒍᖕᓂ ᐃᓅᓯᖅᑲᑦᑎᐊᕐᓗᓂ, ᐱᓕᕆᑎᑕᐅᑦᑕᕆᐊᓛᑦ ᐊᔪᕈᓐᓇᐃᖅᐸᓪᓕᐊᓕᑐᐊᖀᖕᒪᑕ ᐱᓕᕆᓂᕐᒥᒃ.

ᐊ. ᖃᐅᔨᒪᔭᖃᖅᐱᑦ ᐊᖓᔪᖅᑳᓂᒃ ᐃᕐᓂᖃᖕᒋᑦᑐᓂᒃ ᐸᓂᖕᒥᓐᓂᒃ ᐃᕐᓂᕆᔪᑦᑐᑦ ᐃᓕᖅᑯᓯᖃᖅᑎᑦᑎᔪᓂᒃ?

ᑭ. ᐄ ᐊᖓᔪᖅᑳᑦ ᐸᓃᓐᓇᖃᕌᖕᒐᒥᒃ ᐃᕐᓂᖃᖕᒋᔅᓱᑎᒃ ᐸᓂᖕᒥᓂᒃ ᐊᖑᑎᑦ ᐱᓕᕆᐊᕆᔪᔭᐃᓐᓂᒃ ᐱᓕᕆᑎᑦᑎᔪᔪᑦ. ᐅᓇ ᐆᒃᑐᑎᒋᓗᒍ ᕿᒧᒃᓯᕌᒃᑯᑦ ᐊᕐᑯᐃᑎᐸᒃᓱᒋᑦ ᐊᒻᒪ ᐊᓯᖕᒋᓐᓂᒃ ᐊᖑᑎᑦ ᐱᓕᕆᐊᖕᒋᓐᓂᒃ.

ᐊ. ᐊᑑᑎᖃᑦᑎᐊᕋᔭᖅᐸ ᓄᑕᕋᕗᑦ ᖃᐅᔨᒪᑎᑦᑎᐊᕈᑉᑎᒋᑦ ᑭᑐᓂᒃ ᐃᓚᖃᕐᒪᖔᑖ?

ᑭ. ᐄ ᐅᑉᓗᒥᐅᓕᖅᑐᖅ ᐱᒻᒪᕆᐅᕗᖅ ᓄᑕᖅᑲᕗᑦ ᖃᐅᔨᒪᑎᑦᓗᒋᑦ ᑐᖅᓱᕋᐅᓯᕐᓂᒃ ᐃᓐᓇᐅᓂᖅᓴᐃᑦᓗ. ᐃᓛᓐᓂᑯᑦ ᐅᔾᔨᕈᓯᔪᐃᑦᑑᒐᑉᑕ ᐃᓚᒐᓗᐊᑉᑎᓐᓂᒃ ᖃᐃᓯᒪᐃᓐᓇᕋᓗᐊᖅᑎᑦᓗᒋᑦ ᐃᓅᓯᓗᒃᑖᑉᑎᓐᓂᒃ. ᐊᑐᒻᒪᕆᒃᑐᖅ ᐱᒻᒪᕆᐅᑉᓗᓂᓗ ᑐᑭᓯᐅᒪᓂᖅ ᐃᓚᑉᑎᓐᓂᒃ ᑭᑑᖕᒪᖔᑖ ᖃᓄᕐᓗ ᑐᖅᓱᕋᓇᐊᖃᕐᒪᖔᑉᑎᒍ.

ᐊ. ᑐᖅᓱᖅᑐᕋᐅᓂᖅ ᐊᑑᑎᖃᖅᐸ ᖃᓂᑦᓕᑐᕋᐅᓕᖅᐹᓕᕐᓇᖅᐸ ᐃᓚᒌᓄᑦ? ᐃᓄᖕᓄᑦ ᐊᑑᑎᖃᑦᑎᐊᖅᐹ ᐱᒻᒪᕆᒋᔭᐅᕚ?

ᑭ. ᐅᖃᐅᑎᓂᐊᕋᑉᑭᑦ ᐱᒻᒪᕆᐅᔪᒥᒃ ᐊᒻᒪ ᓯᓕᔪᒥᒃ. ᐊᒥᓯᕐᔪᐊᕐᓂᒃ ᐃᓚᖃᕐᒪ ᐊᔾᔨᒌᖕᒋᑐᔾᔪᐊᕐᓂᒡᓗ ᑐᓱᖅᐸᒃᓱᒋᑦ. ᐃᓚᓗᒃᑖᒃᑲ ᖃᐅᔨᒪᔭᒃᑲ ᑐᓱᖅᐸᒃᑲᑉᑭᑦ ᐊᐤᕙᓇᓚᐅᒑᑐᑦ ᑐᖅᓱᖅᓱᒍ. ᐃᓚᒌᖕᓂᖅ ᑐᖅᓱᕋᑐᕋᐅᑎᓂᖅ ᖃᓂᒡᓕᕚᑦᓕᕈᑎᒋᑦᑕᕋᑉᑎᒍ. ᐃᑲᔪᕐᓂᖃᕐᒪᑦ ᓯᓇᒥᐊᒥᒃ ᐊᐱᕆᔭᕆᐊᖃᓕᕌᖕᒐᒪ ᐊᒻᒪᓗ ᐊᐱᖅᑯᖅᑑᑦᓗᐊᒥᐊᖅᓱᒋᑦ ᑐᓐᓂᐊᖕᒋᑦᓗᖓᓗ ᑲᖖᒍᓯᖕᒋᑦᓗᖓᓗ. ᐃᓚᒌᓐᓂᖅ ᖃᓂᑐᖅᐅᕚᓕᕐᓇᒪᑦ.

ᐊ. ᖃᑉᓗᓈᑦ ᑎᑭᑉᐸᓕᐊᓕᕌᖅᑎᓪᓗᒋᑦ, ᐊᔪᕿᖅᑐᐃᔩᓪᓗ, ᓂᐅᕕᖅᑏᓪᓗ ᑐᑭᓯᐊᕙᓚᐅᖅᐸᑦ ᑐᖅᓱᕋᐅᓯᕐᓂᒃ

ᑭ. ᐊᐅᓚᔨᒐᒪ ᓂᐅᕕᖅᑏᑦ ᑎᑭᑉᐸᑦᓕᐊᓕᕌᖅᑎᓪᓗᒋᑦ ᓂᐅᕕᕐᕕᒡᓗ ᐅᒃᑯᐃᓕᕌᖅᑎᓪᓗᒍ ᑕᒫᓂ ᐊᕐᕕᐊᓂ. ᐊᑖᑕᕗᑦ ᐊᖑᑏᑦ ᑎᓇᒐᓂᐊᓂᒃ ᐊᒡᔭᖅᑭᓱᓚᐅᕐᒪᑕ ᐊᑎᓕᐅᖅᓱᑎᒡᓗ. ᐊᒻᒪ ᐃᒃᓯᕋᕐᔪᐊᕋᓗᐃᑦ ᓄᓇᓕᕋᓛᓄᑦ ᑎᑭᑉᐸᓚᐅᕐᒪᑕ ᐊᐅᔭᒃᑯᑦᓗ ᐅᑭᐅᒃᑯᑦᓗ. ᐅᖃᖃᑎᖃᖅᐸᒃᓗᑎᒃ ᐊᖓᔪᖅᑳᑉᑎᓐᓂᒃ ᐃᓕᑦᑎᕙᑦᓕᐊᕙᓚᐅᕐᒪᑕ.

ᒪᑎᐅᑕ ᓱᓗᕌᕚᒃ

ᐊᐱᖅᓱᖅᑕᐅᒪᑦ ᐅᐸᓗᐊ
ᓴᕐᒋᓇᖕᕕᒃ 2012

ᐊ. ᖃᓄᖅ ᑐᖅᑯᕋᖅᑐᕋᐅᓂᖅ ᐊᑑᑎᖃᖅᐸ?

ᑭ. ᐊᑐᕐᓚᓇᓚᐅᖅᑐᑦ ᐃᑯᐋᓪᓛᑦ ᐊᑖᑕᕐᑎᐊᓇᓚᐅᖅᑕᕐᒪ ᐊᑖᑕᕐᑎᐊᕐᓗᐊᕕᒋᖕᒋᑲᓗᐊᖅᑯᒍ ᐊᓈᓇᒪ ᑎᒍᐊᖅᓯᒋᓚᐅᕐᒪᒍ, ᑎᒍᐊᖅᓯᐊᑕ ᓄᑕᕋᖕᒋᑦ ᑐᖅᑯᕋᓗᓇᒃᓴᓚᐅᕋᑉᑭᑦ ᑕᐃᒃᑯᐊ ᑕᒫᓂᑦᑐᑦ ᐊᕕᐊᕐᒥᐅᑎᑐᑦ ᑐᖅᑯᕋᐅᓯᖕᒐᑦ ᐊᑐᖕᒋᓇᑉᑎᒍ ᐊᕙᓂᖅᓕᑎᒍᑦ ᐊᕐᓇᕐᕕᒋᓚᐅᖅᑕᒃᑲ ᐸᓂᖕᒋᑦ ᐊᒻᒪ ᐊᓂᒃᓴᓇᓚᐅᖅᑯᒋᑦ ᐃᕐᓂᖕᒋᑦ ᑕᐃᒪᓐᓇ ᑐᖅᑯᕋᖅᐸᒃᑲᑉᑭᑦ ᐅᐸᓗᒥᒍᑦ ᓱᓕ ᐃᓅᒪᓂᒃ ᒪᑦᑑᒃ ᑲᖕᒋᖅᓱᓂᕐᒥ.

ᐊ. ᑐᓴᐅᒪᕕᑦ ᓴᐅᓂᕉᓂᒃ?

ᑭ. ᐄ ᖃᐅᔨᒪᔭᕋ; ᓴᐅᓂᖃᕋᒫᕐᓛᑦ. ᐃᓐᖑᑕᕐᒪ ᑖᒃᑯᐊ ᓄᑕᕋᐃ ᓴᐅᓂᕆᓇᔭᖅᑕᒃᑲ.

ᐊ. ᐅᓇ ᑐᑭᓯᓂᓗᒃᑕᕋ ᑐᖅᑯᕋᐅᓯᖅ ᖃᓄᖅ ᐊᑐᖅᑕᐅᓯᓚᐅᕐᒪᖔᑦ?

ᑭ. ᓴᐅᓂᖅ ᑐᑭᖕᒐ ᐊᔾᔫᖕᒋᒪᑦ. ᐊᕕᐊᑦ ᓄᓇᓕᖖᒍᓚᐅᒪᑦ ᑲᖕᒋᖅᓱᓂᕐᒥᑦ ᓱᕗᑦᓕᐅᑉᓗᓂ. ᐃᓪᓗᓕᓘᕐᔪᓪᓗ, ᓇᐅᔮᑦᓗ ᐊᒻᒪ ᓴᑦᓕᖅ ᑐᖅᑯᕋᐅᓯᖕᒋᑦ ᐊᔾᔨᕌᖕᒪᑕ. ᐃᓐᖑᑕᕋ ᑕᐃᒪ ᓄᑕᕋᖅᑖᖅᐸᑦ ᓴᐅᓂᕆᕙᕋ, ᑕᐃᒪᓐᓇᐃᑉᐸᓚᐅᖅᑐᖅ ᑕᐃᑉᓱᒪᓂ.

ᐊ. ᑐᖅᖢᕋᕐᓂᖅ ᐊᕐᓇᓄᑦᑐ ᐊᖑᑎᓄᑦᑐ ᐊᔾᔨᒌᖏᑉᐸ?

ᑭ. ᐄ ᐊᒥᓱᕐᔪᐊᕐᓂᒃ ᐊᔾᔨᒌᖏᓂᓕᒃ. ᐊᕐᓇᐃᑦ ᐅᔪᑮᓛᓯᐃᑦᑑᒻᒪᑕ (ᑐᖅᖢᕋᐅᓯᐅᒻᒪᑦ ᐊᕐᓇᐅᑉ ᐊᓂᐊᑕ ᐊᑐᔫᔮ ᓇᔮᑕ ᓄᑕᕋᐃᓄᑦ). ᑐᖅᖢᕋᕋᑉᑭᑦ ᐊᓂᒪ ᓄᑕᕋᖏᑦ ᐃᙳᑕᓇᒐᑉᑭᑦ, ᐊᕐᓇᐃᑦ ᑕᐃᒪᓐᓇ ᐊᑐᔫᔮᓂᒃ. ᐊᓈᓇᑦᑎᐊᕋ ᐅᑯᓯᒃᓴᓕᖕᒥᐅᑕᐅᖕᒪᑦ ᐃᓕᑦᑎᕙᒋᓂᑯᒋᒐᑉᑯ ᐊᑐᖅᐸᒃᖢᒋᑦᑐ ᐅᑉᓗᒥᒎᑦ.

ᐊ. ᑭᑐᓂᒃ ᐊᑎᖃᖅᐱᑦ ᐊᒻᒪ ᖃᑉᐱᓂᒃ ᐊᑎᖃᖅᐱᑦ?

ᑭ. ᐊᑕᐅᓯᒨᓐᓇᕐᒥᒃ ᐊᑎᖃᖅᑐᖓ. ᒪᑦᑮᓐᓂᒃ ᐊᖓᔪᖃᓚᐅᕐᒪ ᐃᓅᔪᓐᓇᐃᓚᐅᕐᒪᓂᒃ ᐃᓅᖏᑎᑦᑐᖓᓱᓕ. ᐅᑐᖅᑲᑮᖅ ᐊᓯᐊᕐᒥᐅᑕᖅ ᖃᒪᓂᔾᔪᐊᕐᒥᐅᑕᖅ ᐃᓕᒋᙱᑦᑕᕋᓗᐊᕗᑦ ᑎᑭᓚᐅᖅᓯᒪᖕᒪᑦ ᐃᒡᓗᓕᒫᕐᔪᖑᑦ ᐅᑉᓚᓗᒃᖢᓂ ᐊᖓᔪᖅᑳᒻᓄᑦ ᖁᕕᐊᓱᒋᐊᖅᓯᒪᑎᑦᑐᒋᑦ, ᐊᑦᑎᖅᑕᐅᔪᒪᓕᕐᓂᖅᖢᓂ.

ᐱᕈᖅᓴᑎᑦᑐᖓ ᐃᒡᓗᓕᒫᕐᔪᖕᒥ, ᐃᖅᑲᐅᒪᔭᕋ ᐅᑉᓚᓗᒃᑎᑦᑐᒍ ᐅᕝᐸᑎᓐᓄᑦ. ᐅᑐᖅᑲᔅᔪᐊᖅ ᖃᐅᔨᒪᙱᑦᑑᒐᓗᐊᖅ ᐊᓈᓇᒐ ᓄᑕᕋᒃᓴᖕᒪᑦ ᐊᑖᑕᒻᓄᑦ ᐅᖃᓚᐅᖅᑑᓐᓂᖅ, "ᓄᑕᕋᖅᑖᒥᒍᑉᓯ ᐅᕝᒻᓂᒃ ᐊᑎᖅᑲᕈᒫᓕᖅᐳᖅ ᐊᔾᔨᒋᑦᑐᐊᕐᓗᓂ ᐃᓅᖅᑲᑦᑖᕈᒫᕐᒪᑦ." ᑕᐃᒪ ᑎᐊᓐᓇ ᐊᑎᖅᑖᓚᐅᖅᑐᖓ ᑭᒪᓕᐊᕐᔪᖕᒥᒃ. ᐱᐅᒋᑐᐊᓚᐅᖅᓯᒪᙱᑦᑕᕋ ᐅᑐᖅᑲᔅᔫᖕᒪᑦ ᓂᐱᕐᓗᒫᑐᐊᖅᖢᓂ ᐃᓅᔪᓐᓇᐃᓚᐅᑐᖅ ᐅᑐᖅᑲᑦᑐᐊᖅᖢᓂ.

ᐊ. ᑐᓴᐅᒪᔭᖅᑲᖅᐱᑦ ᐊᑎᖅᑖᕈᐊᖏᑦᑐᒥᒃ ᐅᕝᕙᔫᕝᕙ ᐊᑎᖅᑖᕈᐊᖅᑐᒥᒃ ᐃᓕᒋᙱᑕᖅᑐᐊᒥᓂᒃ?

ᑭ. ᓇᐅᒃ, ᑕᒪᓐᓇ ᑐᓴᐅᒪᙱᑕᕋ, ᑖᒻᓇ ᐅᖃᐅᓯᕆᓚᐅᖅᑕᕋ ᐅᑐᖅᑲᖅ ᐊᕝᕙᓇᓚᐅᖅᑕᕋ ᐆᒃᑑᑎᑦᑎᐊᔾᔫᒪᑦ. ᐃᓕᒋᖏᒃᑲᓗᐊᕐᐸᑎᒍ

ᓄᓇᖃᑎᒋᖕᒋᕐᓘᒍᓗ ᐊᐱᕆᔭᖃᑐᓚᐅᕐᒪᑦ ᐊᖓᔪᖃᒃᑲᓂᒃ ᐊᑦᑎᖃᑕᐅᓱᐊᖅᓘᓂ. ᐋᓈᓇᑦᑎᐊᕋ ᐊᖏᓚᐅᕐᒪᑦ ᐊᑦᑎᕐᑯᑉᓗᓂᐅᒃ ᐊᑎᖃᑖᓚᐅᖅᐸᖓ ᐅᕐᑲᓚᐅᕐᒪᑦ ᐃᓅᕐᑲᑦᑖᕐᓂᐊᕋᒪᕗᖅ ᐃᓅᓯᕐᑲᑦᑎᐊᕐᓗᖓᓗ. ᐃᓐᓇᐃᑦ ᐃᓯᒪᓕᐅᖅᑎᐅᕙᓚᐅᕐᒪᑕ ᐃᓅᓯᕐᒥᒃ.

ᓄᑕᕋᓛᖅ ᐃᓕᖕᓂᒃ ᐊᑦᑎᖃᑕᐅᐸᑦ, ᑎᒍᓗᒍ ᓯᕗᓪᓕᖅᐹᒥᒃ ᑕᑯᖕᓂ ᐅᕐᑲᐅᔾᔪᕋᔭᖅᑕᐃᑦ ᐊᖏᕈᓯᐅᖅᑐᑦ ᖃᓄᖅ ᐃᓅᓯᕐᑲᕐᑯᖕᒪᖕᓖᓃ. ᑎᐊ'ᓇ ᐱᓯᓚᐅᒪᑕᑐᑦ, ᑕᐃᒪᓐᓇᐃᒪᑦ ᓱᓕ ᐅᑉᓗᒥᒧᑦ ᐃᓄᐃᑦ ᐃᓚᖏᓐᓄᑦ. ᐃᓖᓐᓂᒃ ᐃᓯᒪᕙᒃᑲᒪ ᖃᓄᖅ ᒪᒃᑯᑦ ᐃᖏᓐᓂᒃ ᐊᑦᑎᖅᑐᐃᕙᖕᒪᖕᓖᑖ ᐃᓅᓯᖅ ᐱᒪᕆᐊᔪᖓᓗᐊᕐᒪᑦ.

ᑕᐃᑉᓯᒪᓂᓕ ᐃᓐᓇᕗᑦ ᐊᖓᔪᖃᕗᑦᔫᓐᓃᑦ ᐊᑦᑎᖅᑐᐃᖏᓐᓇᖅᐸᓚᐅᕐᒪᑕ ᓄᑕᖅᑖᖅᑐᕐᑲᕌᖕᖓᑦ. ᐅᑉᓗᒥᐅᓕᖅ ᐊᔾᔾᔩᓕᕐᒪᑦ ᐃᓐᓇᐅᓕᖅᑐᑎᒍᑦ ᐅᑉᓗᒥ ᕿᐅᕆᒪᒐᓗᐊᖅᓘᑕ ᓇᓗᓕᕋᑉᑕ ᖃᓄᐃᓕᐅᕐᓂᒥᒃ. ᓇᓗᓇᖏᑐᖅ ᑭᓯᒪ ᑕᒪᑐᒥᖓ ᐃᓯᒫᓗᒃᑐᑑᖏᓐᓇᒪ.

ᐊ. ᑐᓴᐅᒪᔭᕐᑲᖏᑉᐱᑦᓕ ᐊᑎᒃᓴᕐᑲᖏᑦᑐᒥᒃ ᐃᓅᓴᖅᑐᒥᒃ ᓄᑕᕋᓛᒥᒃ?

ᑭ. ᖃᐅᔨᕙᒃᑐᖓ ᐃᓖᓐᓂᒃᑯᑦ ᐊᑎᖅᑲᖏᑐᑦ ᓄᑕᕋᓛᑦ ᑎᑭᐅᑎᔭᐅᕙᖕᒪᑕ ᐃᓅᓴᕐᓂᑰᔫᑦ. ᐅᑉᓗᒥᐅᓕᖅ ᐃᓄᐃᑦ ᓇᓗᕙᓕᕐᒪᑕ ᑭᑐᓂᒃ ᐊᑦᑎᖅᓯᓂᕐᒪᖕᓖᕐᒦᒃ. ᐃᓇᐅᔩᑦ ᒪᒃᑯᒃᑐᓂᒃ ᐊᔪᕿᖅᑐᐃᖕᖏᓗᐊᓕᕐᒪᑕ, ᐱᓕᕆᐊᕆᔭᕆᐊᕐᑲᖅᑕᑉᑎᓐᓂᒃ ᓴᒃᑯᑦᑎᓯᒪᓕᕋᑉᑕ. ᐃᓚᖏ ᒪᒃᑯᒃᑐᑦ ᖃᐅᔨᒪᑎᑕᐅᕙᒃᑑᖓᓗᐃᑦ ᑕᐃᒪᓐᓇ ᐅᕙᑎᑐᑦ ᐃᓕᑦᑎᑎᑕᐅᓐᓂᒃᑯᑦ.

ᓇᓪᓕᒍᓯᒃᐸᒃᐳᖓ ᐅᓪᒍᐊᖅᓘᖓᓗ ᒪᒃᑯᒃᑐᕗᑦ ᐃᓕᓐᓂᐊᖅᑎᖏᓐᓇᐸᑎᒍ ᑕᒪᒃᑯᓂᖓ ᐱᒪᕆᐅᔪᓂᒃ ᐃᓅᓯᕐᒧᑦ ᑐᕌᖅᑐᓂᒃ. ᓇᓗᓇᖏᒻᒪᑦ ᑭᑐᓂᒃ ᐊᐱᕆᓂᐊᒪᖕᓖᒥᒃ ᓇᓗᑦᑕᕐᒪᑕ. ᑕᐃᑉᓯᒪᓂᓕ ᓄᓇᓕᕋᓛᒥᐅᑕᐅᕙᓚᐅᕋᑉᑕ ᓇᓗᓇᖅᐸᓚᐅᖏᒪᑦ ᐅᑉᓗᒥᑐᑦ.

ᐊ. ᖃᐅᔨᒪᔭᖃᖕᒋᑉᐱᑦᑕ ᐊᑦᑎᖅᑕᐅᓯᒪᕕᒌᖅᑐᒥᒃ ᐃᓅᓚᐅᖅᑳᖅᑎᓐᓇᒍ ᓄᑕᕋᓛᖅ?

ᑭ. ᐄ ᐃᓚᖕᒋᑎᒍᑦ ᐊᑦᑎᑕᐅᓯᒪᕕᒌᓚᐅᖅᑐᒍᑦ ᐃᓅᖅᑳᖅᑎᓐᓇᑕ. ᐊᑦᑎᖅᑕᐅᕕᒌᖅᓯᒪᓚᐅᕋᒪᓕ ᑕᐃᒪᓐᓇ ᐅᑐᖅᑲᖅ ᐅᖃᐅᓯᕆᓚᐅᖅᑕᕋ ᐊᑎᖅᑖᕈᐊᓚᐅᕐᓂᕐᒪᑦ. ᐊᖓᔪᒋᓚᐅᖅᑕᕋᓗᐊᒃᑲ ᐃᓅᓚᐅᕐᓂᖕᒋᒻᒪᓂᒃ ᑖᒪᓐᓇ ᖃᐃᓚᐅᓂᕐᒪᑦ ᐊᑦᑎᖅᑕᐅᓱᐊᖅᕗᓂ ᐅᖃᕐᓂᖅᕗᓂᓗ, "ᐃᓅᖃᑦᑖᕐᓂᐊᕐᒪᑦ ᐊᑦᑎᑕᐅᔪᒪᔪᖓ," ᐊᓈᓇᒪ ᓄᑕᕋᒃᓴᕆᑎᑦᑐᓂᖓ ᓯᓕ.

ᐊ. ᓄᑕᕋᐅᑎᑦᑐᑎᑦ ᐱᕈᖅᐸᓪᓕᐊᑎᑦᑐᑎᑦ ᐃᓕᓐᓂᐊᖅᑎᑕᐅᓚᐅᖅᐱᑦ ᐊᑎᕐᓂᒃ?

ᑭ. ᓄᑕᕋᐅᑎᑦᑐᖓ ᐱᕈᖅᓴᑎᑦᑐᖓ ᖃᐅᔨᒪᓚᐅᖅᑐᖓ ᐃᓐᓇᐅᑉ ᐊᑎᐊᓂᒃ ᐊᑦᑎᖅᑕᐅᓯᒪᒐᒪ. ᐊᑕᐅᓲᓐᓇᕐᒥᒃ ᐊᑎᖃᖅᑐᖓ ᐊᑎᕆᔭᕋᓗ ᑕᑯᕙᒃᕗᒍ ᖃᑯᑎᒃᑯᑦ, ᐊᖑᑎᕋᐅᔭᕘᓚᐅᕐᒪᑦ ᐅᑐᖅᑲᐅᑉᓗᓂᓗ. ᐱᐅᒋᓗᐊᓚᐅᙱᑕᕋ ᖃᓄᐃᓕᐅᕐᓂᕐᓗ ᐊᔪᖅᕈᖓ ᐊᑎᕋ ᐊᔾᔭᕈᓂᖅ ᐊᔪᓚᐅᕋᑉᑯ. ᖃᓄᓗᒃᑖ ᐅᕙᒻᓄᑦ ᐅᖃᔪᓚᐅᕐᒪᑦ ᐃᓂᖁᓇᐃᓖᖅᕗᓂ ᐱᐅᒋᓚᐅᙱᑕᕋ.

ᐊ. ᖃᐅᔨᓯᒪᕕᑦ ᑭᓇᒥᐊᒥᒃ ᐊᑎᓕᔭᕐᒥᓂᒃ ᐃᑲᔪᖅᑕᐅᔪᒥᒃ?

ᑭ. ᑖᒃᑯᐊᑐᐊᑦ ᐃᓐᓇᕆᔭᐅᔪᑦ ᐊᑦᑎᖅᑐᐃᕙᓚᐅᕐᒪᑕ ᓄᓇᓕᕋᓛᖑᕙᒃᑎᑦᑐᑕ. ᐊᓈᓇᑦᑎᐊᕋ ᐃᓯᒪᑕᐅᕙᓚᐅᕐᒪᑦ ᐅᖃᐅᔾᔪᐃᕙᒃᕗᓂᓗ ᓯᕗᓂᕐᒧᑦ ᖃᓄᐃᓐᓂᐊᕐᓂᑉᑎᓐᓂᒃ. ᐅᖃᐅᔾᔪᖅᐸᓚᐅᕐᒪᖓ ᐊᑦᑎᖅᑐᐃᒥᐊᖅᑕᖁᖕᒋᕐᕗᓂᒐ ᐊᒥᓲᓗᐊᖅᑐᓂᒃ ᓄᑕᖅᑭᐅᓕᕈᒪ ᑎᑭᖅᑕᐅᖅ ᑕᐃᒪᓐᓇ ᐅᖃᐅᔾᔪᖅᐸᓚᐅᕐᒪᒍ. ᐅᖃᖅᐸᓚᐅᕐᒪᑦ ᐊᑦᑎᖅᓯᓂᕉᖅ ᐱᒻᒪᕆᐅᒪᑦ

ᐃᓅᑎᐊᕐᓂᕐᒧᑦ ᐊᑕᖕᒪᑦ ᑕᐃᒪᓐᓇᒥᐊᖅ ᐱᔭᐅᔭᕆᐊᖃᖏᒻᒪᑦ. ᐅᖃᖅᐸᓚᐅᕐᒪᑦ ᐅᔨᕈᓯᑦᑎᐊᕆᐊᕐᓗᑕᒎᖅ ᐊᑦᑎᖅᑐᐃᑦᑕᕈᒫᖅᐳᒍᑦ ᑭᑐᒥᐊᓂᒡᓗ ᐊᑦᑎᖅᓯᕙᖏᑦᓗᑕ ᑭᓯᐊᓂ ᐃᓐᓇᕐᒧᑦ ᐊᐱᓚᔭᐅᒍᑉᑕ ᐊᑦᑎᖅᑕᐅᔪᒪᔪᒧᑦ ᐊᑦᑎᖅᓯᔪᓐᓇᕋᑉᑕ ᐃᓚᒋᙱᑕᑉᑎᓐᓂᒃ. ᐅᖃᐅᑎᕙᓚᐅᕐᒪᑎᒍᑦ ᐃᓅᓯᖅᐳᙵᒎᖅ ᐋᖅᑭᒃᓱᖅᐸᑮᖅᓯᒪᖕᒪᑦ ᐃᓅᓚᐅᖅᑳᑎᓐᓇᑕᓘᓐᓃᑦ ᐊᑦᑎᓯᔪᒪᒍᑉᑕᒎᖅ ᐃᓚᒋᙱᑕᑉᑎᓐᓂᒃ ᐊᐱᓚᖄᕐᓗᑕ ᑭᓯᐊᓂᐅᖕᒪᑦ ᐃᓐᓇᓇᔭᐅᔪᓂᒃ. ᑕᒪᓐᓇ ᐱᒻᒪᕆᐅᒻᒪᑦ ᐊᑦᑎᖅᑐᐃᓂᖅ ᐊᖏᖅᑕᐅᔭᖐᖓᒥᒃ ᑭᓯᐊᓂ ᐊᑦᑏᓯᕗᖕᒪᑕ ᐃᓚᒋᙱᑕᒥᓐᓂᒃ. ᑕᐃᒪᓐᓇᐃᓚᐅᕐᒪᑦ ᑕᐃᑉᓯᒪᓂ.

ᐊ. ᖃᐅᔨᒪᔭᖃᖅᐱᑦ ᐃᓅᓯᒃᑐᐊᕐᔪᖕᒥᒃ ᐊᑎᖃᖅᐸᑦ ᐊᕐᓇᒥᒃ, ᑖᒻᓇ ᐊᖑᑎᓐᓈᖅ ᐊᕐᓇᑐᑦ ᐃᓕᖅᑯᓯᖃᕋᔭᖅᐸ ᐊᓐᓄᕌᕋᓗᐃᓂᒃ ᐊᕐᓇᑦ ᐊᑐᖅᐸᒡᓗᓂ?

ᑭ. ᖃᐅᔨᒪᔭᖃᖏᑐᖓ. ᐊᓂᑯᓗᒐ ᓂᐊᖁᕐᓗᖕᒥᒃ ᐊᑎᖃᕐᒪᑦ ᐊᓈᓇᑦᑎᐊᓐᓂᒃ ᐊᑎᖃᕐᒪᑦ ᐊᒻᒪ ᐃᓅᓵᒥᒃ ᑯᕝᕕᓚᓂᖃᖅᓱᓂ. ᓂᐊᖁᕐᓗᖕᒥᒃ ᐊᑎᖃᕐᒪᑦ ᐊᓈᓇᑦᑎᐊᒻᓂᒃ ᐊᑦᑎᖅᓯᒪᖕᒪᑦ ᐊᑦᑎᖅᑕᐅᔪᒪᓚᐅᕐᒪᑦ ᐊᖑᑕᐅᓗᓂ. ᐃᓐᓇᐃᑦ ᖃᐅᔨᒪᔫᔭᖅᐸᓚᐅᕐᒪᑕ ᐊᕐᓇᖅ ᓄᑕᕋᒃᓴᔪᖅ ᖃᐅᔨᒪᔭᐅᕙᓚᐅᕐᒪᑦ ᓄᑕᕋᑖᖅ ᐃᓅᖄᖅᑎᓐᓇᒍ ᐊᕐᓇᐅᓂᐊᕐᒪᖔᑦ ᐊᖑᑕᐅᓂᐊᕐᒪᖔᓘᕝᕙ.

ᐊᓈᓇᑦᑎᕋ ᖃᐅᔨᒪᓚᐅᕐᒪᑦ ᓄᑕᕋᑖᖅ ᐊᖑᑕᐅᓂᐊᕐᒪᑦ ᐊᑎᖅᑖᕈᐊᓚᐅᕐᒪᑦ. ᑕᐃᒪ ᐊᓂᑯᓗᒐ ᐃᓅᓵᖑᓕᖅᐳᖅ. ᐃᓐᓇᐅᓕᖅᑐᑦ ᐅᑉᓗᒥ ᐅᕙᖕᒫᒡᓛᑦ ᖃᐅᔨᒪᑦᑕᕈᓐᓇᐃᕐᑉᑕ ᓯᓇᑖᕐᓂᐊᕐᒪᖔᑦ ᓄᑕᕋᒃᓴᔪᖅ, ᓯᕗᓕᕗᑦ ᖃᐅᔨᒪᔪᕐᔪᐊᖑᓚᐅᕐᒪᑕ ᐃᓅᓯᐅᑉ ᒥᒃᓵᓄᑦ.

ᐊ. ᖃᐅᔨᒪᔭᖃᖅᐱᑦ ᐊᖓᔫᖄᓂᒃ ᐃᕐᓂᖃᖏᑦᑐᓂᒃ ᐸᓂᖕᒥᓐᓂᒃ ᐃᕐᓂᓕᔪᑐᑦ ᐃᓕᖅᑯᓯᖃᖅᑎᑦᑎᔪᓂᒃ?

ᑭ. ᐄ ᑕᐃᒪᓐᓈ ᐱᒐᔪᓚᐅᖅᑐᑦ ᑕᐃᑉᓯᒪᓂ. ᐊᓂᑯᓗᒐᓗ ᐃᓅᓵᖅ ᐹᓗ ᐊᖑᑎᑐᐊᖑᓚᐅᕐᒪᓂᒃ ᐅᕙᑉᑎᓐᓂ ᑕᓪᓕᒪᓂᒃ ᐊᕐᓇᑕᖃᖅᖢᓂ. ᑕᓪᓕᒪᐅᑉᓗᑕ ᐊᕐᓇᐅᓚᐅᕋᑉᑕ. ᐊᓈᓇᒪ ᐱᕈᖅᓴᓚᐅᕐᒪᑎᒍᒃ ᓄᑲᕆᓚᐅᖅᑕᕋᓗ ᓯᑖᓇ ᖃᓄᒥᐊᖅ ᐱᓕᕆᔪᓴᑉᓗᓂᑎᒍᒃ ᐊᖑᑏᓇᒡᓛᑦ ᐱᓕᕆᐊᖏᓂᒃ ᐊᔪᙱᕐᑯᓗᐊᒍᑦ. ᐊᓈᓇᒐ ᒪᖃᐃᑉᐸᓚᐅᕐᒪᑦ ᑐᒃᑐᑯᒥᓗ ᐋᒃᑐᖅᐸᒃᖢᒍ ᐊᖑᑎᑐᒥᐊᖅ ᐱᓕᕆᕙᓚᐅᕐᒪᑦ.

ᐄ ᑕᐃᒪᓇ ᐱᕙᓚᐅᖅᑐᑦ. ᐊᖑᑏᓇᒡᓛᑦ ᒥᖅᓱᕐᓇᐸᓚᐅᕐᒪᑕ ᒥᖅᓲᑎᑕᖃᖏᑎᓪᓗᒍ. ᐊᒡᒐᒧᐃᓇᖅ ᒥᖅᓯᐸᒃᑎᓪᓗᑕ ᐊᖑᑏᓇᒡᓛᑦ ᐳᐊᓗᓕᐅᕐᓂᕐᒥᒃ ᐊᔪᙱᓚᐅᕐᒪᑕ. ᐊᖑᑏᑦ ᒪᖃᐃᑉᐸᓚᐅᕐᒪᑕ ᖃᐅᑕᒫᑦ ᐃᓐᓇᕈᕌᖓᑕ. ᐃᓚᖏᓇᒡᓛᑦ ᒥᖅᓱᕐᓇᖅᐸᓚᐅᖅᑐ ᐃᖕᒥᓐᓂᒃ ᐊᓐᓄᕌᓕᐅᖅᐸᒃᖢᑎᒃ ᒪᖃᐃᖃᑦᑖᕌᖓᒥᒃ.

ᐊᑖᑕᒐᓗ ᐊᖓᒐᓗ ᒪᖃᐃᑎᓪᓚᕆᐅᓚᐅᕐᒪᓂᒃ, ᐊᖓᒐ ᒥᖅᓱᕐᓇᑎᐊᓚᐅᕐᒪᑦ ᐊᓈᓇᑦᑎᐊᕐᒪ ᐃᓕᓐᓂᐊᖅᑎᑉᐸᓚᐅᕐᒪᒍ. ᐊᓈᓇᑦᑎᐊᕐ ᐱᓕᕆᔪᓴᐃᑦᑎᐊᖅᐸᓚᐅᕐᒪᑦ. ᒪᖃᐃᖃᑦᑕᕌᖓᒥᒃ ᓄᑖᓂᒃ ᐊᓕᖅᑎᓕᐅᖅᐸᓚᐅᕐᒪᑦ ᐊᑎᒋᓕᐅᖅᐸᒃᖢᓂᓗ ᐊᒥᕐᓂᒃ ᐱᑕᓵᖅᑕᒥᓐᓂᒃ. ᐊᖓᒐ ᐊᔪᙱᑦᑎᐊᓚᐅᕐᒪᑦ ᓯᓇᒥᐊᓂᒃ.

ᐊ. ᐊᑑᑎᖃᑦᑎᐊᕋᔭᖅᐸ ᓄᑕᕋᕗᑦ ᖃᐅᔨᒪᑎᑦᑎᐊᕈᑉᑎᒋᒃ ᑭᑐᓂᒃ ᐃᓚᖃᕐᒪᖔᑖ?

ᑭ. ᐄ, ᑕᐃᒪᓐᓇᐃᑐᖅ. ᓄᑕᕋᒃᑲ ᐅᖃᐅᑎᕙᒃᑲᑉᑭᑦ ᐃᙳᑕᒃᑲᓗ ᑭᑐᓂᒃ ᐃᓚᖃᕐᒪᖔᑉᑕ ᖃᓄᓂᕐᓗ ᑐᖅᖢᕋᓂᐊᕐᒪᖓᑖ,ᑭᓯᐊᓂ ᐊᔪᕐᓇᖅᑐᔾᔮᕆᓕᕐᒪᑦ ᐅᑉᓗᒥᐅᓕᖅᑐᖅ. ᑐᖅᖢᕋᐅᓯᕐᓂᒃ ᐊᑐᓗᐊᕈᓐᓇᐃᓪᒪᑕ ᑭᑐᓗᒃᑖᑦ ᐊᑎᕐᒥᑎᒍᑦ ᖃᑉᓗᓈᑐᑦ ᐊᑐᖅᑕᓕᓪᒪᑕ. ᑕᐃᑉᓯᒪᓂ ᐱᕈᖅᓴᑎᑦᑐᖓ ᑐᖅᖢᕋᑐᕋᐅᖏᓐᓇᖅᐸᓚᐅᖅᑕ. ᐅᖃᐅᑎᕙᒃᑲᑉᑭᑦ ᑭᑐᓂᒃ ᐃᓚᖃᕐᒪᖔᑉᑕ ᐅᖃᐅᑎᑉᓗᒋᑦᓗ ᖃᐅᔨᒪᓕᑐᕐᐅᒃᑲᓐᓂᕐᓗᑎᒃᓗ ᖃᓂᑐᕐᐅᓕᒃᑲᓐᓂᕐᓂᐊᕐᒪᑕ.

ᐊ. ᑐᖅᖢᕋᖅᑐᕋᐅᓂᖅ ᐊᑑᑎᖃᖅᐸ ᖃᓂᓪᓕᑐᕋᐅᓕᖅᐹᓕᕐᓇᖅᐸ ᐃᓚᒌᓄᑦ?

ᑭ. ᐄ, ᖃᓂᓪᓕᕚᓕᕈᑎᒋᕙᓚᐅᕋᑉᑎᒍᓕ ᐃᓄᒃᑎᒍᑦ ᐊᑐᖅᐸᑎᑦᓗᑎᒍ ᖃᐅᑕᒫᑦ. ᐃᓄᐃᑦ ᐃᓚᒌᒃᑐᑦ ᐃᑲᔪᖅᑐᕋᐅᒥᓐᓇᖅᐸᓚᐅᕐᒪᑕ ᖃᓄᓗᒃᑖᖅ. ᐃᑲᔪᖅᑕᐅᔪᖃᕆᐊᖃᖅᐸᑦ ᖃᖓᒥᐊᑦᑎᐊᖅ ᐊᑐᐃᓇᐅᕙᓚᐅᕋᑉᑕ ᐃᑲᔪᓂᐊᕐᓗᑕ, ᑭᓯᐊᓂ ᐅᑉᓗᒥ ᐃᓪᓗᔪᐊᕐᒥᐅᑕᐅᓕᖅᑎᑦᓗᑕ ᐃᓚᑉᑎᓐᓄᑦ ᓅᓐᓃᑦ ᐅᑉᓚᓗᔪᐃᑦᑑᓕᕋᑉᑕ. ᐃᓄᐃᑦ ᐃᓚᒌᑦ ᑲᑐᔾᔨᕙᓚᐅᕋᓗᐊᕐᒪᑕ ᐱᓕᕆᐊᒃᓴᓂᒃ ᐊᖏᔪᓂᒃ ᒪᒃᑯᓂᖓᕋᓗᒃ ᐋᒃᑐᖅᓗᑎᒃ ᑐᒃᑐᓂᒃ ᓇᑦᑎᕐᓂᓪᓗ ᐊᒥᓱᓂᒃ ᐱᑕᖅᐸᑕ. ᑕᐃᒪᓐᓇᐃᖏᓕᕋᑉᑕ, ᐃᑲᔪᖅᑐᕋᐅᐸᙱᓕᕋᑉᑕ. ᑕᒪᓐᓇ ᐊᓯᔾᔨᓗᐊᓂᖅᐹᖑᖃᑕᐅᔪᖅ ᐃᓕᖅᑯᓯᑉᑎᓐᓂ.

ᐊ. ᖃᑉᓗᓈᑦ ᑎᑭᑉᐸᓪᓕᐊᓕᔮᖅᑎᑦᓗᒋᑦ, ᐊᔪᕿᖅᑐᐃᔩᓪᓗ, ᓂᐅᕕᖅᑏᑦᓗᑐᑭᓯᐊᕙᓚᐅᖅᐸᑦᑐᖅᖢᕋᐅᓯᕐᓂᒃ

ᑭ. ᓇᐅᖑᖅᑰᖅ; ᑐᑭᓯᐊᓚᐅᖏᑐᑦ ᑐᖅᖢᕋᐅᓯᑉᑎᓐᓂᒃ ᐃᓄᐃᑦ ᑲᑉᐱᐊᓱᒃᐸᓚᐅᕐᒪᑕ ᖃᑉᓗᓈᓂᒃ ᑕᐃᑉᓱᒪᓂ. ᐃᓪᓗᓕᒑᕐᔪᖕᒥ ᖃᑉᓗᓈᓂᒃ ᑕᑯᕙᓚᐅᕋᒪ ᐳᑭᖅᑕᓕᖕᓂᒃ, ᓂᐅᕕᖅᑎᓂᒃ, ᐃᒃᓯᕋᕐᔪᐊᕐᓂᒃ, ᓇᔭᖕᓂᒃ ᐊᒻᒪ ᓈᓚᒃᑎᓂᒃ; ᑖᒃᑯᐊᑐᐊᑦ ᖃᑉᓗᓈᖑᓚᐅᕐᒪᑕ ᓄᓇᓕᖕᒥ.

ᓈᓐᓯ ᑕᔅᓯᐅᖅ
ᐊᐱᖅᓱᖅᑕᐅᒪᑦ ᐅᑉᓗᐊ
ᐊᑯᓪᓕᕈᕐᕕᒃ 2012

ᐊ. ᑐᓴᐅᒪᕕᑦ ᓴᐅᓂᕇᓂᒃ?

ᑭ. ᓇᐅᒃ, ᖃᐅᔨᒪᙱᑕᕋ ᑖᒻᓇ ᖃᓄᖅ ᐊᑐᖅᑕᐅᕙᖕᒪᖔᑦ. ᑐᓴᐅᒪᖏᓐᓇᑉᑯ ᑐᖅᓱᕋᐅᓯᖅ. ᐃᒻᒪᖄ ᑕᑉᐹᓂᕐᒥᐅᓄᑦ ᐊᑐᖅᑕᐅᕙᒃᑐᖅ. ᐃᓚᖏᓐᓂᒃ ᓱᓕ ᑐᑭᓯᐅᒪᖏᓐᓇᒪ.

ᐊ. ᑐᖅᓱᕋᕐᓂᖅ ᐊᕐᓇᓄᓪᓗ ᐊᖑᑎᓄᓪᓗ ᐊᔾᔨᒌᖏᑉᐸ?

ᑭ. ᐄ, ᐊᕐᓇᖅᑎᒌᑦ ᐊᒻᒪ ᐊᖑᑎᖅᑎᒌᑦ ᐅᖃᐅᓯᕆᒐᑉᑎᒍ. ᑖᒃᑯᐊ ᑐᖅᓱᕋᐅᔩᑦ ᑐᑭᓯᐊᔭᒃᑲ ᑭᓯᐊᓂ ᐊᑐᖅᑕᐅᓗᐊᖅᑑᔭᕈᓐᓇᐃᖅᒪᑕ ᐅᑉᓗᒥᐅᓕᖅᑐᖅ. ᐊᒥᓲᖏᑦᑐᓐᓈᑦ ᑐᖅᓱᕋᖅᑐᕋᐅᓕᖅᒪᑕ, ᐅᕙᑉᑎᑐᑦ ᐊᕐᓇᖅᑎᒃᑲᓗ. ᓴᑮᓛᓂᖅᓘᓐᓃᑦ ᐊᑐᖅᑕᐅᓗᐊᕈᓐᓇᐃᖅᒪᑦ ᑕᐃᑉᓱᒪᓂᑐᑦ. ᐅᑉᓗᒥ ᑐᖅᓱᕋᖅᑐᓂᒃ ᑐᓴᓗᐊᖅᐸᙱᓕᕋᒪ.

ᐊ. ᑕᐃᑉᓱᒪᓂ ᐊᑏᑦ ᐊᑐᖅᓱᒥᑦ ᐱᖅᑎᑖᖅᑎᑕᐅᕙᓚᐅᖅᐸᑦ?

ᑭ. ᖃᐅᔨᒪᖏᑐᖓ ᐊᑏᑦ ᐊᑐᖅᑕᐅᕙᓚᐅᖅᒪᖔ ᐱᖅᑎᑖᕈᑕᐅᕙᓚᐅᖅᒪᖔ. ᐊᖓᔪᖅᑳᕗᑦ ᓂᕈᐊᔪᓚᐅᖅᒪᑕ ᑭᑐᓂᒃ ᐅᐃᑖᕐᓂᐊᕐᒪᖔᑉᑕ. ᒪᒃᑯᒃᑐᑦ ᐃᓱᒪᖅᓱᖅᐸᓚᐅᖏᒻᒪᑕ ᐊᖓᔪᖅᑳᖏᑦ ᐃᓱᒪᑕᐅᓚᐅᖅᒪᑕ. ᐃᓛᓂᓪᓘᓐᓃᑦ ᖃᐅᔨᒪᕙᓚᐅᖏᓐᓇᑉᑕ ᑭᑐᒃ ᐅᐃᑖᕇᓂᐊᕐᒪᖔᓃᒃ.

ᐊ. ᑭᑐᓂᒃ ᐊᑎᖃᖅᐱᑦ ᐊᒻᒪ ᖃᑉᐱᓂᒃ ᐊᑎᖃᖅᐱᑦ?

ᑭ. ᐊᖕᒐᔪᖅᑳᒪ ᑲᑉᓗᑎᐊᕐᒥᒃ ᐊᑦᑎᓚᐅᕐᒪᖔ, ᑕᐃᒪᙵᓂᑦ ᐊᑎᓇᒐᑉᑯ. ᐃᓄᐃᑦ ᑖᒃᓯᒥᒐ ᐊᑐᔪᖕᒪᑕ ᐅᕙᒻᓄᑦ. ᑯᕝᕕᓇᔭᐅᒐᓂᒃᑲᒪ ᐊᔪᕿᖅᑐᐃᔨᓄᑦ ᓈᓐᓯᒥᒃ ᐃᓄᐃᑦ ᐊᑐᖅᑕᓕᓚᐅᖅᑐᑦ ᐃᓛᓂᑯᑦ ᑲᑉᓗᑦᑎᐊᕐᒥᒃ.

ᐊ. ᐊᖕᒐᔪᖅᑳᑦ ᐊᑦᑎᖅᑐᐃᓂᖓᑦ ᐊᔾᔭᕈᖅᓯᒪᓕᖅᐸ?

ᑭ. ᐄ; ᐃᒻᒪᖄ ᐃᓄᐃᑦ ᐊᕐᓇᖏᑦ ᓄᑕᕋᖅᑖᕌᖓᒥᒃ ᑕᓴᒪᓂ ᖃᑉᓗᓈᓂ, ᐃᓚᖏᑦ ᒪᒃᑯᓂᖅᓴᐃᑦ ᐊᕐᓇᑦ ᐊᑦᑎᕐᓂᒃᑕᖏᑦᑐᑦ. ᐃᓚᖏᑦ ᐱᖅᑲᓐᓈᕐᒥᖕᓂᒃ ᐊᑦᑎᖕᓂᐸᒃᑐᑦ ᐅᖃᖃᑎᒋᖅᑳᖅᖢᒋᑦ. ᐃᓄᐃᑦ ᐊᑦᑎᕐᓂᒃᑕᓕᕐᒪᑕ ᓄᓇᖅᑲᑎᒋᖕᒋᑕᕐᒥ'ᓂᒃ ᐊᑦᑎᖅᑕᐅᓯᒋᓂᒃᑳᖕᒐᒥᒃ, ᐊᒻᒪ ᐃᓚᖏᑦ ᐊᒥᓱᔾᔪᐊᕐᓂᒃ ᐊᑎᖃᖅᑕᓕᖅᖢᑎᒃ.ᓯᕗᓕᓇᓚᐅᖅᑕᒃᑲᓕ ᐊᒥᓱᔾᔪᐊᕐᓂᒃ ᐊᑎᖃᖅᐸᓚᐅᖕᒋᒻᒪᑕ.

ᐊ. ᐊᖕᒐᔪᖅᑳᑦ ᓂᕈᐊᖅᓯᖅᐸᓚᐅᖅᐸᑦ ᓄᑕᕋᖓᑦ ᑭᓇᒥᒃ ᐊᑎᖃᕐᓂᐊᖅᒪᖔᑦ?

ᑭ. ᐊᖕᒐᔪᖅᑳᕗᑦᓗ ᓴᑭᕗᑦᓗ ᐊᑦᑎᖅᑐᐃᕙᓚᐅᕐᒪᑕ, ᒪᒃᑯᒃᑐᑦ ᐃᓯᒪᖅᓯᖅᐸᓚᐅᖕᒋᑦᑐᑦ ᓄᑕᕋᖓᑦ ᑭᓇᒥᒃ ᐊᑎᒐᕐᓂᐊᕐᒪᖔᑦ.

ᐊ. ᖃᐅᔨᒪᔭᖅᑲᖕᒋᑉᐱᑦᑕ ᐊᑦᑎᖅᑕᐅᓯᒪᕗᒌᖅᑐᒥᒃ ᐃᓅᓚᐅᖅᑳᖅᑎᓐᓇᒍ ᓄᑕᕌᖅ?

ᑭ. ᐄ, ᐃᓚᖏᑦ ᐃᓅᓚᐅᖅᑳᖅᑎᓐᓇᒋᑦ ᐊᑎᖅᑖᑦᑕᔪᔪᑦ. ᐃᓅᔭᕌᖓᑦ ᓄᑕᕌᖅ ᐊᕝᕖᑕ ᐊᑎᐊ ᐊᑐᖅᖢᒍᑦ ᑐᖅᖢᕋᑕᐅᕙᒃᑐᖅ.

ᐊ. ᓄᑕᕋᐅᑎᓪᓗᑎᑦ ᐱᕿᖅᐸᓪᓕᐊᑎᓪᓗᑎᑦ ᐃᓕᓐᓂᐊᖅᑎᑕᐅᓚᐅᖅᐱᑦ ᐊᑎᕐᓂᒃ?

ᑭ. ᓇᐅᒃ, ᐃᓕᓐᓂᐊᖅᑎᑕᐅᓚᐅᖏᑦᑐᖓ ᐊᑎᒻᓂᒃ; ᐊᓈᓇᒪ ᐊᑦᑎᓚᐅᕐᒪᖓ ᐃᓄᒃᑐᑦ ᑎᐊ'ᐊ ᑐᖅᖁᕋᖅᑕᐅᓯᓚᐅᖅᑐᖓ ᐱᕿᖅᓴᑎᓪᓗᖓ.

ᐊ. ᖃᐅᔨᓯᒪᕕᑦ ᑭᓇᒥᐊᒥᒃ ᐊᑎᓇᔭᕐᒥᓂᒃ ᐃᑲᔪᖅᑕᐅᔪᒥᒃ?

ᑭ. ᐄ, ᐊᑦᑎᖅᑕᐅᔭᕖᖕᒐᑉᑕ ᐊᕝᕙᖅᑖᖅᖁᑕ ᐱᑦᑎᐊᕐᑯᐃᓇᖅᐸᒃᑲᑉᑎᒍ. ᐃᓄᐃᑦ ᐃᓚᖏᑦ ᐅᒃᐱᕐᓂᕐᒥᒃ ᖃᐅᔨᒪᓕᕐᒪᑕ ᑕᐃᒪ ᖃᑉᓗᓈᑐᑦ ᐊᑏᓂᒃ ᐊᑐᐃᓇᖅᐸᓕᖅᐳᑦ.

ᐊ. ᐃᓅᓯᒃᑐᐊᕐᔫᑉᐸᑦ ᐊᕐᓇᐅᑉ ᐊᑎᐊᓂᒃ ᐊᑦᑎᖅᓯᒪᒃᐸᑦ ᐊᕐᓇᐅᑉ ᐃᓕᖅᑯᓯᐊᓂᒃ ᐃᓕᖅᑯᓯᕐᑲᕋᔭᖅᐹ ᐊᒻᒪ ᐊᕐᓇᐅᒍᒥ ᐊᖑᑎᐅᑉ ᐊᑎᐊᓂᒃ ᐊᑎᕐᑲᕆᒥ ᐊᖑᑎᑐᑦ ᐃᓕᖅᑯᓯᕐᑲᕋᔭᖅᐹ?

ᑭ. ᐃᓚᖏᑦ ᓄᑕᖅᑲᑦ ᐱᙳᐊᔪᖕᒪᑕ ᐱᙳᐊᒥᐊᓂᒃ ᐱᕿᐸᓪᓕᐊᑎᓪᓗᒋᑦ, ᖃᓄᐃᖏᑦᑐᖅ ᐊᕐᓇᖅᓯᐅᑕᐅᐸᑦ ᐊᖑᑎᓯᐅᑕᐅᐸᔫᓐᓃᑦ. ᐊᓈᓇᒪ ᐱᕿᖅᐸᓪᓕᐊᑎᓪᓗᖓ ᐃᓕᓐᓂᐊᖅᑎᐸᓪᓚᐅᕐᒪᖓ ᐊᔪᕐᖃᖅᓯᒥᐊᔪᓚᐅᖅᑕᕋ. ᐃᓚᖏᑦᑕᐅᖅ ᐃᓅᓯᒃᑐᐊᕐᔪᐃᑦ ᐊᑖᑕᒥᓂ ᐊᓃᕐᑲᑕᐅᕙᖕᒪᑕ ᐃᓕᓐᓂᐊᖅᖁᑎᒃ ᕿᒧᒃᓯᕋᕐᓂᕐᒥᒃ ᐃᓪᓗᓕᐅᕐᓂᕐᒥᓪᓗ ᐊᖑᑎᑦ ᐱᕙᒐᐃᓐᓂᒃ.

ᐊ. ᑕᐃᒪ ᐃᓅᓯᒃᑐᐊᕐᔪᐃᑦ ᐊᑖᑕᒥᓂᒃ ᐃᓕᓐᓂᐊᖅᑎᑕᐅᕙᓚᐅᖅᐹᑦ ᐊᒻᒪ ᓂᕕᐊᖄᔭᐃᑦ ᐊᓈᓇᒥᓐᓃᑦ?

ᑭ. ᐊᖕᒐᔾᔭᖅᑳᑉᑕ ᐃᓕᓐᓂᐊᖅᑎᑉᐸᓚᐅᕐᒪᑎᒍᑦ ᖃᐅᔨᒪᔭᓇᐊᖅᑲᖅᑕᑉᑎᓐᓂᒃ

ᐱᓯᖅᓴᑎᓪᓗᑕ. ᐊᑖᑕᑉᑕ ᐃᓅᓯᒃᑐᐊᕐᔪᐃᑦ ᐃᓕᓐᓂᐊᖅᑎᕐᓱᒋᑦ ᐃᓕᑦᑎᕖᓪᓕᐊᕙᓚᐅᕐᒪᑕ ᑕᐅᑐᖕᓂᒃᑯᑦ ᐱᓕᕆᓂᒃᑯᓪᓗ ᐃᑲᔪᖅᓱᑎᒃ ᐊᑖᑕᒥᓐᓂᒃ ᖃᒧᑎᓕᐅᕋᓗᒃᓱᑎᒃ ᖃᓄᕐᓗ ᕿᒧᒃᓯᕋᔪᖕᒪᖔᑖ. ᓄᑕᖅᑲᑦ ᐃᓚᖏᑦ ᑐᑭᓯᐅᒪᑎᐊᖅᐸᓚᐅᖅᑐᑦ ᐃᓅᓯᕐᒥᒃ ᐊᕐᓇᐅᑉᓗ ᐊᖑᑎᐅᑉᓗ ᐱᓕᕆᐊᖏᓐᓂᒃ.

ᐊ. ᑐᖅᓱᕋᖅᑐᕋᐅᓂᖅ ᐊᑑᑎᖃᖅᐸ ᖃᓂᓪᓕᑐᕋᐅᓕᖅᐹᓕᕐᓇᖅᐸ ᐃᓚᒌᓄᑦ?

ᑭ. ᐄ, ᓄᑕᖅᑲᕗᑦ ᐅᖃᐅᑎᑦᑕᕋᓐᓂ ᐃᓚᖃᕐᒪᖔᑖ ᑭᑐᓂᒃ ᖃᓄᕐᓗ ᑐᖅᓱᕋᕆᐊᖃᕐᒪᖔᑖ ᑐᖖᒐᒋᑐᕋᐅᕖᓪᓕᖅᐸᒃᑐᑦ. ᐊᐱᖅᑯᑎᖃᕈᓐᓇᐃᖅᓱᑎᒃ ᖃᓂᒡᓕᑐᕋᐅᕖᓕᖅᐸᒃᑐᑦ ᐃᓚᒌᖕᓂᕐᒥᓐᓂᒃ ᖃᐅᔨᑦᑎᐊᕌᖕᒐᒥᒃ. ᑕᐃᒃᑯᐊ ᐃᓐᓇᕐᓂᒃ ᓈᓚᒃᐸᒃᑐᑦ ᑐᑭᓯᐅᒪᓂᖅᓴᐅᕙᖕᒥᔪᑦ ᐃᓚᒌᓂᕐᒥᒃ.

ᐊ. ᖃᑉᓗᓈᑦ ᑎᑭᑉᐸᓕᐊᓕᓵᖅᑎᓪᓗᒋᑦ, ᐊᔪᕿᖅᑐᐃᔩᓗ, ᓂᐅᕕᖅᑏᓪᓗ ᑐᑭᓯᐊᕙᓚᐅᖅᐸᑦ ᑐᖅᓱᕋᐅᓯᕐᓂᒃ?

ᑭ. ᐃᓚᖏᑦ ᖃᑉᓗᓈᑦ ᐃᓕᓐᓂᐊᖅᑎᑕᐅᓯᒪᔪᑦ ᑐᑭᓯᐊᕙᓚᐅᖅᑐᑦ. ᐃᓄᐃᓪᓗ ᖃᑉᓗᓈᓪᓗ ᑐᑭᓯᐊᑦᑐᕋᐅᓚᐅᖏᒻᒪᑕ ᑕᑯᑐᕋᐅᑦᑕᓕᓵᕋᒥᒃ ᑭᓯᐊᓂ ᑐᑭᓯᐊᑐᕋᐅᓕᖅᐸᓪᓕᐊᓕᓚᐅᖅᑐᑦ ᑭᖑᓂᖓᒍᑦ. ᐃᒻᒪᖄ ᐊᔪᕿᖅᑐᐃᔩᑦ ᐃᓚᖏᑦ ᑐᑭᓯᐊᓂᖅᓴᐅᕙᓚᐅᖅᑐᑦ ᐃᑲᔪᖅᐸᓚᐅᕐᒪᑕ ᓄᑕᖅᑲᓂᒃ ᐊᑦᑎᖅᑐᐃᑉᓗᑎᒡᓗ ᖃᑉᓗᓈᑐᑦ. ᐃᒻᒪᖄ ᐃᓚᖏᑦ ᐃᖅᑲᐅᒪᔪᑦ.

ᑐᖅᓗᑭᐅᓰᑦ

ᐱᖕᒐᔪᖕᒐᑦ

ᖃᓄᖅ ᑐᖅᓗᑭᐅᓰᑦ ᐊᑐᖅᑕᐅᓚᐅᖅᐸᑦ

ᓚᐅ ᐃᓐᓇᐅᓂᖅᓴᖅ ᐋᒻᒪᖅ
ᐊᐱᖅᓱᖅᑕᐅᒻᒪᑦ ᐅᑉᓗᐊ
ᓴᒡᒋᓇᕝᕙᒃ 2012

ᐊ. ᐱᐅᓂᖅᓴᐅᕚ ᐊᑦᑎᑦᓚᒃᓯᓐᓇᖕᒋᑦᓗᒍ ᐃᓅᔪᓐᓇᐃᓰᓗᐊᖅᑎᑦᓗᒍ ᐃᓄᒃ?

ᑭ. ᓯᕗᓕᕗᑦ ᓯᓚᑐᔩᓚᐅᕐᒪᑦ ᑐᐊᕕᖕᒋᕐᓱᑎᒃ ᓲᓇᒥᐊᓂᒃ ᐃᓕᕐᒃᑯᓯᕐᑲᓚᐅᕐᒪᑦ; ᑐᐊᕕᖕᒋᕐᓱᑎᒃ ᐱᒻᒪᕆᐅᔪᓂᒃ ᐃᓅᓯᕐᒧᑦ ᑐᕌᕐᒃᑐᓂᒃ ᐃᓅᕙᓚᐅᕐᒪᑦ. ᐃᓅᔪᓐᓇᐃᕐᒃᑐᕐᑲᕌᖕᒐᑦ ᐅᕐᑲᐅᑎᔭᐅᕙᓚᐅᕋᑉᑕ ᐊᑦᑎᑦᓚᒃᓯᓐᓇᕐᑯᔭᐅᖕᒋᕐᓱᓂ ᑭᓯᐊᓂ ᐅᑭᐅᕐᒃ ᐊᑕᐅᓯᕐᒃ ᕐᑳᖕᒋᕐᒃᐸᑦ. ᐊᒻᒪ ᐃᓚᒋᔭᐅᔪᑦ ᐊᐱᕆᕐᒃᑳᕐᓗᒋᑦ ᐱᕐᑯᔭᐅᕙᓚᐅᕐᒃᑐᒧᑦ ᐃᓚᒋᖖᒋᑕᑉᑎᓐᓂᒃ ᐊᑦᑎᕐᒃᓯᓂᐊᕈᑉᑕ.

ᐊ. ᑭᓇᒥᐊᕐᒃ ᐊᑦᑎᕐᒃᓯᔪᓐᓇᕐᒃᐹ, ᐅᕝᕙᔫᕝᕙ ᑕᒪᓐᓇ ᐃᓐᓇᐃᑦ ᐱᓕᕆᐊᕆᔭᕆᐊᕐᑲᕐᒃᐸᔾᔮᒃ?

ᑭ. ᐊᑖᑦᑖᕐᓗᕗᑦ ᐃᓅᓚᐅᕐᒃᐸᑕ, ᕐᑲᐅᔨᒪᓇᔭᕐᒪᑕ ᑭᑐᓂᒃ ᐃᓚᕐᑲᕐᒪᖕᖔᑉᑕ ᑭᑐᓂᒃ ᐊᑦᑎᕐᒃᑐᐃᓇᔭᕐᒪᖕᖔᑉᑕ ᓇᓗᓇᔾᔭᖕᒋᑦᑐᑦ. ᑕᐃᒪ ᐊᕐᓇᐃᑦ ᓄᑕᕐᑲᕐᒃᑖᕐᑳᖕᒐᒥᒃ ᐃᓐᓇᕆᔭᒥᓐᓄᑦ ᐊᐱᕆᑦᑕᕆᐊᕐᑲᕐᓗᐊᕐᒪᑕ ᕐᑲᐅᔨᒪᔪᓂᒃ. ᑕᐃᒪᓐᓇ ᐊᑦᑎᕐᒃᑐᐃᕙᓚᐅᕐᒪᑕ.

ᐊ. ᕐᑭᒻᒦᑦᑕᐅᕐᒃ ᐊᑎᕐᑲᕆᐊᕐᑲᓴᖕᒪᑕ, ᐃᓅᑉ ᐊᑎᐊᓂᒃ ᐊᑦᑎᕐᒃᓯᔪᓐᓇᕐᒃᐸᑦ ᕐᑭᒻᒥᒥᒃ?

ᑭ. ᕐᑭᒻᒥᑎᑦ ᐊᑦᑎᕈᓐᓇᕐᒃᑕᑎᑦ ᐃᓱᒪᖕᓂᒃ ᐃᓅᑉ ᐊᑎᓇᓴᓗᐊᕐᒃᐸᒍ ᓈᒪᒃᑐᕐᒃ. ᐱᖕᒐᓱᓂᒃ ᐊᕐᕕᓂᓕᖕᒧᑦ ᕐᑭᒻᒥᕐᑲᕈᒪ ᐊᑎᕐᑲᓗᒃᑖᓴᔭᕐᒪᑕ. ᐊᑎᕐᒥᓐᓂᒃ ᐃᓕᑕᕐᒃᓯᔪᓐᓇᕐᒃᓯᓗᑎᒡᓗ.

ᐊ. ᕐᑲᓄᕐᒃ ᕐᑲᐅᔨᔪᓐᓇᕐᒃᐳᖕᒐ ᐃᓅᔪᓐᓇᐃᕐᒃᓯᒪᔪᕐᒃ ᐊᑎᕐᒃᑖᕈᐊᐸᑦ ᐅᕙᑉᑎᓐᓂ?

ᑭ. ᓄᓕᐊᕇᑎᒍᑦ ᐅᕐᑲᕐᑲᑎᕐᑮᒃᑕᕆᐊᕐᑲᓴᑉᑕ ᓲᓇᓗᒃᑖᓂᒃ, ᑕᐃᒪ ᐊᖕᒋᕐᑲᑎᕐᑮᒃᑑᓗᐊᕐᒃᐳᒍᑦ ᐊᑦᑎᕐᒃᓯᓂᐊᕈᑉᑕ ᓄᑕᓴᑉᑎᓐᓂᒃ.

ᐊᑦᑎᖅᓯᔪᒪᒍᕕᑦ ᐃᓅᔪᓐᓇᐃᓯᒪᓕᖅᑐᒥᒃ ᐃᓚᒋᔭᐅᔪᑦ ᐃᓐᓇᕆᔭᐅᔪᓪᓘᓐᓃᑦ ᐊᐱᕆᔭᖅᑐᖃᔭᒃᑲᑎᑦ. ᐅᖃᓘᑎᒃᑰᖕᒋᑐᑦ ᑕᑯᓗᒋᑦ ᑮᓇᕐᒧᑦ ᐅᕐᑲᕐᑲᑎᒋᑦᑎᐊᓂᐊᕋᖕᓂ ᐊᖕᒋᕐᑲᑎᒋᓗᒋᑦᓗ.

ᐊ. ᐃᓅᔪᓐᓇᐃᖅᓯᒪᔪᖅ ᖃᓄᖅ ᓂᕈᐊᕋᔭᖅᐸ ᐊᑦᑎᖅᑕᐅᓯᐊᕐᓗᓂ? ᐃᓚᒋᑉᐸᔾᔪᑉ ᐱᕐᑲᓐᓈᕆᑉᐸᔾᔪᓪᓘᓐᓃᑦ ᐅᕝᕙᓘᕝᕙ ᐊᓯᐊᒍᑦ?

ᑭ. ᑎᑭᑕᐅᓚᐅᙱᑎᓪᓗᑕ ᐊᔾᕿᖅᑐᐃᔨᕋᓗᖕᓄᑦ ᑲᕙᒪᓄᓪᓗ ᐃᓄᒃᑎᒍᑦ ᐊᑦᑎᖅᑐᐃᔪᑐᖅᑕᐅᓚᑉᑕ. ᐱᖅᑲᓐᓈᖅᑲᕈᕕᑦ ᐃᓅᔪᓐᓇᐃᖅᓯᒪᔪᒥᒃ ᐊᑦᑎᕈᐊᓂᕈᖕᓂ ᐊᐱᕆᓇᔭᕋᕕᑦ ᐃᓚᖕᒋᓐᓂᒃ. ᐊᖕᒋᕋᔭᕐᒪᑦ ᐱᖅᑲᓈᕆᔭᐃᑦ ᐊᑦᑎᕈᐊᕈᖕᓂ.

ᐊ. ᖁᕝᕕᐊᓱᖕᒋᓐᓇᔭᕆᕙ ᑭᓇᑭᐊᖅ ᐊᑦᑎᖅᑕᐅᓐᓂᕈᒥ ᑖᒃᑯᓇᓂ ᐅᕙᒍᖅᑲᕈᐊᖕᒋᑦᓗᓂ?

ᑭ. ᐊᐱᕆᒥᐊᓈᕈᕕᑦ ᐃᓄᐃᑦ ᐊᖕᒋᕐᓂᐊᖅᑐᑦ. ᐃᓄᒃᑎᒍᑦ ᓇᓪᓕᒍᓯᓪᒍᓛᖑᓚᑉᑕ. ᐊᒥᓱᑎᒍᑦ ᐱᑦᑎᐊᖅᑐᕋᐅᕝᑲᑉᑕ ᐊᓯᑉᑎᓐᓂᓪᓗ ᐃᒃᐱᒍᓱᑦᑎᐊᖅᓗᑕ, ᑕᐃᒪ ᐃᓄᐃᑦ ᐊᒥᓲᓂᖅᓴᐃᑦ ᐊᐱᕆᔭᐅᒍᒥᒃ ᓈᒪᒃᓴᕋᔭᖅᑐᑦ ᐃᓚᒋᔭᙳᑦ ᐊᑎᖅᑕᐅᓯᐊᖅᐸᑦ.

ᐊ. ᖃᓄᖅᑕ ᐊᑦᑎᖅᓯᓂᖅ ᐅᑎᖅᑎᑦᑎᔭᓐᓇᖅᐸ ᑕᐃᑉᓱᒪᖓ ᐃᓅᙵᑎᓕᖅᑐᒥᒃ?

ᑭ. ᐃᓄᐃᑦ ᐊᖑᑎᖕᒋᑦ ᐊᑦᑎᑐᐃᕙᖕᒋᒪᑕ, ᑕᒪᓐᓇ ᐊᖅᓇᐅᑉ ᐱᓕᕆᐊᕆᖕᒪᒍ. ᓄᓕᐊᖑᔪᖅ ᓄᑕᕋᕆᔭᐅᔪᕐᓘᓐᓃᑦ ᐊᑦᑎᖅᓯᔪᒪᒍᓂ ᐊᐱᕆᖅᑳᓱᖅᒪᑦ ᐃᓇᕆᔭᐅᔪᒥᒃ. ᓄᑕᖅᒥᓐᓂᒃ ᐊᑦᑎᖅᓂᒃᐸᖕᒪᑕ ᐃᓐᓇᖕᒋᑕ ᐊᑎᕆᖅᑯᔭᙳᓂᒃ. ᐅᒃᐱᕈᓱᒃᑲᒪ ᐃᓄᒃ ᐅᑎᖅᐸᖕᒪᑦ

ᐃᓅᓯᓐᓇᐃᕐᓯᒪᓕᕋᓗᐊᕐᓗᓂ ᐊᑦᑎᕐᑕᐅᔭᕌᖓᒥ. ᓇᖕᓕᒍᓱᒃᑲᑉᑕ ᐃᓚᑉᑎᓐᓂᒃ ᐱᕐᑲᓐᓈᑉᑎᓐᓂᖕᓗ ᖃᐅᔨᓴᐃᓇᕐᓗᑎᓗ ᖃᓄᐃᖕᒋᑲᓗᐊᕐᒪᖕᒑᑖ.

ᒪᑎᐅᑕ ᓱᓗᕌᔫᒃ

ᐊᐱᖅᓯᖅᑕᐅᒪᑦ ᐅᑉᓗᐊ
ᓴᒡᒋᓇᖖᕕᒃ 2012

ᐊ. ᑖᒻᓇᓕ ᓄᑕᕋᓛᖅ ᐊᑦᑎᖅᑕᐅᓯᒪᑉᐸᑦ ᐃᓚᒋᓚᐅᖅᑕᒥᒃ ᐱᑦᑎᐊᖅᑕᐅᕚᑦᓕᖅᐸᓚᐅᖅᐸ ᐊᑏᐊ ᐱᔾᔪᑕᐅᑉᓗᓃ?

ᑭ. ᐄ, ᓯᕗᓕᓇᓚᐅᖅᑕᒃᑲᓕ ᐱᖅᑯᓯᕐᑲᓚᐅᕐᒪᑕ ᓄᑕᕋᓛᖅ ᐊᑦᑎᖅᑕᐅᐸᑦ ᐊᑎᓇᓚᐅᖅᑕᖓᑐᑦ ᐱᖅᑯᓯᕐᑲᕐᕕᐅᖏᒃᑐᖅ. ᐊᕝᕙᓇᓚᐅᖅᑕᕋ, ᐅᑐᖅᑲᐅᓚᐅᖅᑐᖅ ᑕᑯᔭᖅᑐᓚᐅᓂᕐᒪᖓ ᐃᓅᓴᖅᑎᑦᓗᖓ ᐅᕐᑲᖅᓱᓂᓗ ᐊᔪᖕᒋᑎᐊᕐᓂᐊᕋᒪᒎᖅ ᓯᓇᒥᐊᓂᒡᓗ ᐱᓕᓇᑦᑎᐊᕈᓐᓇᕐᓗᖓ ᐊᒻᒪ ᕐᑭᓯᓕᓇᔪᓐᓇᑦᑎᐊᕐᓗᖓ ᐊᑐᖅᑕᐅᕙᖕᒪᑕ ᐊᖑᑎᓄᑦᓗ ᓄᑕᖅᑲᓄᑦᓗ. ᐃᒡᓗᔪᐊᖅᑲᖅᑳᑎᓐᓇᒍ ᓂᕐᔪᑎᑦᐊᒥᖕᒋᑦᐊᑐᖅᑕᐅᕙᒃᑎᑦᓗᒋᑦᐃᒡᓗᔪᐊᒥᐅᑕᐅᓚᐅᖅᑳᖅᑎᓐᓇᑕ ᓂᕐᔪᑎᑦ ᕐᑭᓯᖕᒋᑦ ᐊᑐᑦᑎᐊᓚᐅᕐᒪᑕ. ᐅᕐᑲᐅᑎᓚᐅᖅᓯᒪᓐᓂᕐᒪᖓ ᐊᔪᖕᒋᑦᑎᐊᕈᒫᕐᒪᒎᖅ ᕐᑭᓯᓕᓇᓂᕐᒥᒃ ᑭᓯᐊᓂ ᐊᐅᓚᓴᖕᒋᑐᖓ ᓄᑕᕋᓛᖑᓚᐅᕐᒪ.

ᐱᕈᖅᓴᑎᑦᓗᖓ ᐊᓈᓇᒐᓗ ᐊᓈᓇᑦᑎᐊᕋᓗ ᓇᑦᓯᑦ ᕐᑭᓯᖕᒋᓐᓂᒃ ᑐᐱᓕᐅᖅᐸᓚᐅᕐᒪᑕ ᐊᒻᒪ ᐅᑭᐅᒃᑯᑦ ᑐᒃᑐᑦ ᐊᒥᖕᒋᓐᓂᒃ ᑐᐱᕐᑲᖅᐸᒃᓱᑎᒃ ᐃᓛᓐᓂᒃᑯᑦ ᐃᒡᓘᒦᐸᒃᓱᑎᒃ. ᑕᐅᑐᒃᐸᓚᐅᕋᑉᑭᒃ ᕐᑭᓯᖕᓂᒃ ᐱᓕᓇᐊᕐᑲᖅᑎᑦᓗᒋᒃ ᓂᕐᑭᓕᐅᖅᑎᑦᓗᒋᒡᓗ ᐃᓚᑉᑎᓐᓂᒃ, ᓂᑉᑯᓕᐅᖅᓱᑎᒃ ᐱᑉᓯᓕᐅᖅᓱᑎᒡᓗ ᓯᓇᒥᐊᓂᒡᓗ ᐱᑕᓇᓴᐅᔪᓂᒃ ᓂᕐᔪᑎᓂᒃ. ᑖᒃᑯᐊᒃ ᐃᓕᑦᑎᕕᕐᔪᐊᖅᓯᒪᒐᑉᑭᒃ ᑕᐅᑐᒃᓱᒋᒃ.

ᐊᖕᒋᑦᓕᕙᑦᓕᐊᑎᑦᓗᖓ ᑐᓯᒋᕙᓚᐅᕋᑉᑭᑦ ᐊᓈᓇᑦᑎᐊᕋᓗ ᐊᕐᓇᕕᒃᑲᓗ ᐊᓈᓇᒐᓗ ᐱᓕᓇᑎᑦᓗᒋᑦ ᕐᑭᓯᖕᓂᒡᓗ ᐊᒥᕐᓂᒡᓗ. ᑕᐅᑐᐸᒃᑎᑦᓗᖓ ᐊᒥᓕᓇᑎᑦᓗᒋᑦ ᐅᓗᒥᓐᓂᒃ ᐊᑐᖅᓱᑎᒃ ᐊᔪᕐᓇᖕᒋᑎᐊᖅᑑᔭᖅᐸᓚᐅᕐᒪᑦ. ᕐᑯᕕᐊᓇᖅᑑᔭᖅᓱᓂᓗ ᐃᓯᒪᕙᓚᐅᕋᒪ ᑎᐊ'ᓇᑐᑦ ᐊᔪᖕᒋᑎᐊᕈᒪᑉᓗᖓ.

ᐊᓈᓇᑦᑎᐊᕋ ᐅᕐᑲᐅᑎᓚᐅᓯᒪᔭᕋ ᐃᓕᑦᑎᔪᒪᑉᓗᖓ

ᕿᓯᓕᕆᓂᕐᒥᒃ. ᓇᑦᑎᐅᑉ ᓯᖅᑯᐊᓂᒃ ᓇᑲᑦᑎᖁᑉᓗᓂᖓ ᐱᓚᖁᓚᐅᖅᓯᒪᖕᒪᒍ ᐅᖃᖅᖢᓂᓗ "ᑎᐊ'ᓇ ᑭᓯᐊᓂ ᐃᓕᑦᑎᓂᐊᕐᕋᕕᑦ ᕿᓯᓕᕆᓂᕐᒥᒃ." ᐱᓂᓗᐃᓇᖅᖢᖓ ᓯᖅᑯᓈᓂᒃ ᓴᓗᒻᒪᑎᐊᕐᓂᓗᒃᖢᒍ ᐱᓕᕆᐊᕆᓚᐅᖅᓯᒪᔭᕋ. ᓱᓇᒥᐊᓂᒃ ᐊᔪᕈᓐᓇᐃᖅᓴᔪᓚᐅᕐᒪᑎᒍᑦ. ᐃᓱᒫᓗᒋᕙᓚᐅᖏᒻᒪᑎᒍᑦᑕᖅᑲᓂᐊᕈᒋᕋᓗᒃᖢᑕᐱᓕᕆᔪᓴᓕᕌᖓᑦᑎᒍᑦ..

ᐊ. ᑭᓇᒥᐊᖅ ᐊᑦᑎᖅᓯᔫᑦᓗᐊᖅᐹ, ᐅᕝᕙᓘᕝᕙ ᐃᓐᓇᐃᑦ ᑭᓯᒥᒃ ᐊᑦᑎᖅᓯᔭᕆᐊᖃᖅᐸᑦ?

ᑭ. ᐅᑉᓗᒥᐅᓕᖅᑐᖅ ᑭᓇᓗᒃᑖ ᐊᑦᑎᖅᓯᑦᑕᓕᕐᒪᑦ ᐊᑎᕆᖁᔭᕐᒥᓂᒃ ᐊᔪᕐᓇᖅᑐᔅᔫᓕᖅ. ᑕᐃᑉᓱᒪᓂ ᐃᓄᐃᑦ ᐃᓚᐃᓇᕐᒥᓐᓂᒃ ᐊᑦᑎᖅᓯᕙᓚᐅᕋᓗᐊᕐᒪᑕ ᐅᕝᕙᓘᕝᕙ ᖁᔭᒋᓯᒪᔭᕐᒥᓐᓂᒃ. ᐃᒻᒪᖄ ᐃᑲᔪᖅᑎᒋᕐᔪᐊᖅᓯᒪᔭᕐᒥᓐᓂᒃ ᐊᑦᑎᖅᓯᕙᓚᐅᖅᑐᑦ. ᑕᒪᓐᓇ ᐊᑦᓚᕈᔅᔪᐊᖅᓯᒪᓕᕐᒪᑦ ᐃᓐᓇᑉᑎᓐᓄᓗ ᑕᑯᔭᐅᔅᔪᐊᖅᓯᒪᑉᓗᓂ ᐊᔅᔭᕈᖅᐸᓕᐊᓂᐊ ᐃᓅᓯᐅᑉ.

ᐅᖃᐅᔭᐅᕙᓚᐅᕋᑉᑕ ᖃᓄᒥᐊᖅ ᐊᑦᑎᖅᑐᐃᖁᔭᐅᖏᔅᖢᑕ ᓄᑕᕋᑉᑎᓐᓂᒃ ᑕᑯᓕᓵᒐᑉᑎᓐᓂᒡᓘᓐᓃᑦ ᐊᑦᑎᖅᑕᐅᓇᓱᒋᔭᑉᑎᓐᓂᒡᓘᓐᓃᑦ, ᑭᓯᐊᓂ ᑕᐃᒪᓐᓇᐃᓕᖅᑐᖅ ᐅᑉᓗᒥ. ᒪᒃᑯᒃᖢᑕ ᐊᑦᑎᖅᓯᓂᐅᔭᓚᐅᖏᓇᑉᑕ ᓄᑕᕋᑉᑎᓐᓂᒃ. ᐊᔪᕐᓇᑦᑐᐊᕕᓚᐅᖅᑐᖅ—ᓈᒪᓚᐅᖏᒪᑦ. ᐊᓈᓇᒪᓗ ᓴᑭᒪᓗ ᓄᑕᖅᑲ ᐊᑎᖅᐸᓚᐅᕐᒪᒋᑦ.

ᐊ. ᖃᓄᐃᑉᐸᓕ ᑭᓇᒥᐊᖅ ᐃᓚᒋᙱᑕᖅᐳᑦ ᐊᑦᑎᖅᓯᓇᔭᖅᐸᑦ ᐃᓚᒋᔭᒻᓂᒃ ᐃᓅᔪᓐᓇᐃᖅᓯᒪᓕᖅᑐᒥᒃ? ᐊᑖᑕᒻᓂᒃ ᐊᓈᓇᒻᓂᒡᓘᕝᕙ ᐃᓅᙱᓕᖅᑐᓂᒃ ᐊᑎᖅᓯᔪᒪᒃᐸᑕ ᖃᐅᔨᑎᑕᐅᖅᑳᕆᐊᖃᕋᔭᖅᐳᖔ? ᖃᓄᕐᓕ ᐱᓇᔭᖅᐳᖓ?

ᑭ. ᐄ, ᑕᒪᓐᓇ ᐱᒻᒪᕆᐅᔪᖅ ᖃᐅᔨᑎᑕᐅᑦᑕᕐᓂᖅ ᐊᑦᑎᖅᓯᔪᒪᔪᓄᑦ

ᐃᓚᒋᔭᐅᖏᑦᑐᓄᑦ, ᐊᖓᔪᖅᑳᓂᒃ ᐊᑦᑎᖅᓯᔪᒪᑉᐸᑕ. ᐊᑦᑎᖁᖏᒃᑯᑉᑭᑦ ᐊᑦᑎᖅᑕᐅᔭᕆᐊᖃᖏᑦᑐᑦ. ᐊᖏᕐᓂᖅ ᐄᓗ ᓇᐅᒡᓗ ᐊᑑᑎᖅᑲᑦᑎᐊᖅᐳᒃ ᐊᑦᑎᖅᓯᓂᐊᕐᓗᓂ.

ᐅᕙᖓᓕ ᐊᐱᕆᔭᐅᔭᕌᖓᒪ ᖁᕕᐊᑦᑕᑕᕋᒪ. ᑭᓇᒥᐊᖅ ᐊᑦᑎᖅᓯᔪᒪᒑᖓᑦ ᕿᐊᓯᙳᓕᕐᓇᖅᓱᓂᓗ ᖁᔭᓕᓐᓇᕐᒪᑦ. ᐅᐃᒋᓚᐅᖅᑕᕋ ᓱᓗᕌᔫᖅ ᐊᑦᑎᖅᑕᐅᔪᒪᑎᑦᓗᒍ ᓴᑦᑕᕐᒥ ᖁᔭᓕᑦᑕᓇᓚᐅᕐᒪ ᐃᓅᔪᓐᓇᐃᖅᓯᒪᓕᓚᐅᕐᒪᑦ ᐅᑭᐅᒥᒃ ᐊᑕᐅᓯᕐᒥᒃ. ᐊᐱᕆᔭᐅᒐᒪ ᕿᐱᓗᒍᓐᓇᙱᓚᐅᖅᑐᖓ ᓱᓗᕌᔫᒧᑦᓗ ᐃᓚᒋᔭᐅᓚᐅᕐᒪᑕ ᐊᑦᑎᖅᓯᔪᒪᔪᑦ ᐊᓈᓇᖓᑕ ᐃᓚᒋᓚᐅᕐᒪᒋᑦ. ᖁᕕᐊᑦᑕᓐᓇᓚᐅᖅᑐᖅ ᐃᓗᒃᑯᑦ ᐃᓱᒪᒃᑯᑦᓗ.

ᐊ. ᐊᑦᑎᖅᓯᒋᐊᖃᖏᑉᐳᖓ ᓄᑕᕋᒻᓂᒃ ᐃᓅᔪᓐᓇᐃᓵᖅᑐᒥᒃ? ᐊᑎᐊ ᐊᑐᕆᐊᑲᓗᐊᖅᐸᑦ ᐃᓅᔪᓇᐃᓵᓗᐊᖅᑎᑦᓗᒍ ᓈᒻᒪᖏᑉᐹ?

ᑭ. ᐄ, ᐱᒻᒪᕆᐅᒪᑦ ᐅᑕᖅᑭᔭᕆᐊᖃᖅᐸᒃᑑᒐᓗᐃᑦ ᐅᑭᐅᒥᒃ ᐊᑕᐅᓯᕐᒥᒡᓘᓐᓃᑦ ᐊᑦᑎᖅᓯᔪᒪᔪᑦ ᐃᓅᔪᓐᓇᐃᖅᓯᒪᓕᖅᑐᒥᒃ. ᐅᑉᓗᒥᐅᓕᖅᑐᖅ ᑕᒪᓐᓇ ᐊᑐᕈᓐᓇᐃᓴᑉᑎᒍ ᐃᓕᖅᑯᓯᐅᓚᐅᖅᑐᖅ ᒪᒃᑯᒃᑐᕗᑦᓗ ᖃᐅᔨᒪᑎᓐᓂᓗᒍᓐᓇᐃᖅᓱᒋᑦ.

ᐊ. ᕿᒻᒦᑦᑕᐅᖅ ᐊᑎᖃᕆᐊᖃᔪᖕᒪᑕ, ᐃᓅᑉ ᐊᑎᐊᓂᒃ ᐊᑦᑎᖅᓯᔪᓐᓇᖅᐳᖔ ᕿᒻᒥᒥᒃ?

ᑭ. ᐊᑖᑕᒐᓕ ᕿᒻᒥᒥᓂᒃ ᐃᓅᑉ ᐊᑏᓂᒃ ᐊᑦᑎᖅᓯᕙᓚᐅᖏᒪᑦ, ᖃᐅᔨᒪᔭᖃᖏᕐᓱᖓᓗ ᑭᓇᒥᐊᒥᒃ ᕿᒻᒥᒥᓂᒃ ᐃᓅᑉ ᐊᑎᐊᓂᒃ ᐊᑦᑎᓂᒃᑐᒥᒃ. ᑕᐃᑉᓱᒪᓂ ᕿᒻᒦᑦ ᐃᓅᔾᔪᑎᑐᐊᕆᕙᓚᐅᕐᐸᑎᒍ ᐱᓕᕆᔨᒋᕐᔪᐊᖅᓱᒋᑦᓗ ᑕᐃᒪ ᓈᒪᓚᐅᖏᑉᐳᖅ ᐃᓄᓂᒃ ᐊᑦᑎᓂᐊᕐᓗᒋᑦ. ᐃᒻᒪᖄ ᐃᓚᖏᑦ ᓄᑕᖅᑖᔪᐃᑦᑐᑦ ᐊᑦᑎᓯᕙᒃᑑᒐᓗᐃᑦ ᐊᖓᔪᖄᒥᓐᓂᒃ.

ᐊ. ᖃᓄᖅ ᖃᐅᔨᔪᓐᓇᖅᐳᖓ ᐃᓅᔪᓐᓇᐃᖅᓯᒪᔪᖅ ᐊᑎᖅᑖᕈᐊᖅᐸᑦ ᐅᕙᑉᑎᓐᓂ?

ᑭ. ᐱᐅᓂᖅᓴᐅᓇᔭᖅᑐᖅ ᐃᓚᒋᔭᐅᔪᑦ ᖃᐅᔨᑎᓚᐅᖅᑳᕐᓗᒋᑦ ᐊᑦᑎᖅᓯᓂᐊᕈᑉᑕ ᐃᓚᒋᓚᐅᖅᑕᖏᓐᓂᒃ. ᐃᓐᓇᕆᔭᐅᔪᖅ ᐊᐱᕆᓗᒍ ᐃᓚᖅᑲᖅᑐᓂᑦ, ᓈᒪᒃᓴᖅᐸᑕ ᐊᑦᑎᖅᓯᔪᓐᓇᖅᑐᑦ.

ᐊ. ᐃᓅᔪᓐᓇᐃᖅᓯᒪᔪᖅ ᖃᓄᖅ ᓂᕈᐊᕋᔭᖅᐸ ᐊᑦᑎᖅᑕᐅᓯᐊᕐᓗᓂ? ᐃᓚᒋᑉᐸᔾᔪᑉ ᐱᖃᓐᓈᕆᑉᐸᒡᔪᓪᓘᓐᓃᑦ ᐅᕝᕙᓘᕝᕙ ᐊᓯᐊᒍᑦ?

ᑭ. ᐊᓈᓇᒐ ᐃᓅᔪᓐᓇᐃᖅᑳᖅᑎᓐᓇᒍ ᐅᖃᓚᐅᖅᓯᒪᖕᒪᑦ ᐊᑦᑎᖅᑕᐅᑦᑕᕈᐊᖕᒋᔅᓱᓂ ᑭᑐᒥᐊᓂᑦ ᐃᓚᒋᖕᒋᑕᒥᓂᑦ. ᐊᑦᑎᖅᑕᐅᔪᒪᑦᑕᓚᐅᖅᒪᑦ ᖃᐅᔨᒪᔭᒥᓂᑦ ᑭᓯᐊᓂ.

ᐊᓈᓇᑦᑎᐊᖅ ᐅᖅᑲᓚᐅᖅᒪᑦ ᐊᓈᓇᒻᓂᑦ ᓄᑕᖅᑖᑦᑕᑕᖅᐸᑦ ᐊᐱᕆᔭᐅᓂᖅᐸᑦ ᐊᑦᑎᖅᑕᐅᔪᒪᔪᒍᑦ ᐊᖏᕆᐊᖅᑲᖅᒪᑦ ᐱᓗᐊᖅᑐᒥᒃ ᐃᓐᓇᐅᑉᐸᑦ ᐅᖅᑲᖅᑐᖅ, ᓴᓪᓗᖕᒋᔅᓱᓂ ᐅᖅᑲᖅᒪᑦ ᑖᒻᓇ.

ᐊ. ᖁᕕᐊᓱᖕᒋᓐᓇᔭᕆᕙ ᑭᓇᑭᐊᖅ ᐊᑦᑎᖅᑕᐅᓐᓂᕈᒥ ᑖᑯᓇᓂ ᐅᕙᒍᖅᑲᕈᐊᖕᒋᑦᓗᓂ?

ᑭ. ᐄ, ᑕᐃᒪᓐᓇᐃᑐᐃᓐᓇᕆᐊᓕᒃᑕᐅᖅ. ᐃᓄᒃᑕᖃᖕᒥᒪᑦ ᐊᑦᑎᖅᑕᐅᔪᒪᖕᒋᑦᑐᓂᒃ ᑭᓇᒥᐊᒍᑦ ᐃᓄᑑᔪᒪᒐᒥᒃ. ᐊᑦᑎᖅᑕᐅᖕᒋᒥᐊᓕᖅᓱᑎᒃ ᐃᓚᒥᓐᓄᓇᓪᓛᑦ.

ᐊ. ᐊᑦᑎᖅᓯᔪᓂ ᐃᓚᒋᔭᕐᒥᒃ ᐃᓅᔪᓐᓇᐃᖅᓯᒪᔪᒥᒃ ᒪᒥᑉᐹᓕᕐᓇᖅᐹ ᐊᑦᑎᖅᑕᐅᑎᓪᓗᒍ?

ᑭ. ᐋᒻᒪᓇᒃ, ᐊᑎᖅᑖᕌᖕᒐᑦ ᐃᓚᒋᓚᐅᖅᑕᑦ ᓴᑐᖅᐸᒃᑲᑉᑎᒍ. ᐃᙳᑕᖅᑲᖅᑐᓂ ᐊᑎᖅᑲᕌᖕᒐᑦ ᐃᓚᒋᓚᐅᖅᑕᒥᒃ ᓴᐃᒻᒪᖅᐹᓕᖅᓇᖅᑐᖅ.

ᐊ. ᖃᓄᖅᓕ ᐊᑦᑎᖅᓯᓂᖅ ᐅᑎᖅᑎᑦᑎᔪᓐᓇᖅᐸ ᑕᐃᑉᓱᒥᖕᒐ ᐃᓅᙱᓕᖅᑐᒥᒃ?

ᑭ. ᐋ, ᐃᓅᙱᓕᖅᑐᖅ ᐊᑦᑎᖁᓐᓂ ᓴᑐᖅᐸᒃᑲᑉᑎᒍ ᐅᑎᖅᐸᖕᒪᑦ ᐅᕙᒍᒥᓄᑦ. ᐅᓇᑐᑦ ᕿᒪᒃᑕᐅᒍᑉᑕ ᐊᐃᔩᔭᖅᑕᕐᒪᑕ. ᑖᒻᓇ ᓴᑐᖅᐸᒃᑲᑉᑎᒍ ᐊᑎᖕᒐ. ᐊᑐᖅᓯᒪᔭᖄᒡᓛᑦ ᐆᓯ ᐊᑦᑎᖁᑉᑯ ᐊᑖᑕᒻᓂᒃ. ᖃᓯᔾᔩᒥᓚᐅᖅᑐᖕᒐ ᓲᕐᓗ ᐊᑖᑕᒐ ᐅᕙᑉᑎᓄᑦ ᐊᐃᔪᖅ. ᓯᓗᖄᔫᒃᑕᐅᖅ ᑕᐃᒪᓐᓇ ᐃᓯᒪᖃᓚᐅᕐᒪᑦ ᓴᑭᓂ ᓇᒡᓕᒋᓚᐅᕐᒪᒍ. ᐅᑎᖅᑑᔭᖅᐸᖕᒪᑕ ᐊᑎᖅᓯᔪᓂ ᐃᓅᔪᓐᓇᐃᖅᓯᒪᓕᖅᑐᒥᒃ.

ᓈᓐᓯ ᑕᔅᓯᐅᖅ
ᐊᐱᖅᓱᖅᑕᐅᒪᑦ ᐅᑉᓗᐊ
ᐊᑯᓪᓕᕈᕐᕕᒃ 2012

ᐊ. ᑖᒻᓇᓕ ᓄᑕᕋᓛᖅ ᐊᑦᑎᖅᑕᐅᓯᒪᐸᑦ ᐃᓚᒋᓚᐅᖅᑕᒥᒃ ᐱᑦᑎᐊᖅᑕᐅᕖᑦᓕᖅᐸᓚᐅᖅᐸ ᐊᑏᐊ ᐱᔾᔪᑕᐅᑉᓗᓃ?

ᑭ. ᓄᑕᕋᓛᖅ ᐊᑦᑎᖅᑕᐅᒃᐸᑦ ᐃᓇᕐᒥᓪᓘᓃᑦ ᐃᓅᔪᓐᓇᐃᖅᓯᒪᔪᒥᒡᓘᓐᓃᑦ ᐃᓛᓐᓂᒃᑯᑦ ᐃᓕᖅᑯᓯᓇᓚᐅᖅᑕᖕᒐᓂᒃ ᐊᑎᐊᑕ ᐃᓕᖅᑯᓯᖃᖅᐸᒃᑐᖅ ᐊᒻᒪ ᐆᒻᒪᓇᖕᓂᖅᓴᐅᓕᖅᓗᓂ. ᓄᑕᕋᓛᖅ ᐊᑭᓴᖅᑐᐃᔩᔭᖅᐸᒃᑐᖅ ᐊᑎᖏᓂᒃ ᐊᔭᕋᔭᓚᐅᕙᐃᓂᒃ ᐊᔪᖕᒋᑎᐊᓕᖅᓗᓂ.

ᐊ. ᑭᓇᒥᐊᖅ ᐊᑦᑎᖅᓯᔫᑦᑐᐊᖅᐹ, ᐅᕝᕙᓘᕝᕙ ᐃᓐᓇᐃᑦ ᑭᓯᒥᒃ ᐊᑦᑎᖅᓯᔭᓇᐊᖅᑲᖅᐸᑦ?

ᑭ. ᒪᒃᑯᒃᑐᑦ ᐅᐸᓗᒥ ᐃᖕᒥᓂᒃ ᐊᑦᑎᖅᓯᑦᑕᓕᕐᒪᑕ ᐊᖕᒐᔪᖅᑳᒥᓐᓂᒃ ᐊᐱᖅᓱᖕᒋᕐᓗᑎᒃ. ᑕᐃᑉᓱᒪᓂ ᐊᓈᑦᑕᖅᑐᐃᑕ ᐱᓕᕆᐊᕆᕙᓕᐅᖅᑕᖕᒋᓐᓂᒃ ᐱᓂᖅᓴᐅᑦᑕᓕᕐᒪᑕ. ᐃᓚᖕᒋᐊᓛᑦ ᐊᒥᓱᓂᒃ ᐊᑎᖃᖅᑕᓕᕐᒪᑕ.

ᐊ. ᖃᓄᐃᑉᐸᓕ ᑭᓇᒥᐊᖅ ᐃᓚᒌᖖᒋᑕᖅᐳᑦ ᐊᑦᑎᖅᓯᓇᔭᖅᐸᑦ ᐃᓚᒋᔭᒻᒥᓂᒃ ᐃᓅᔪᓐᓇᐃᖅᓯᒪᓕᖅᑐᒥᒃ? ᐊᑖᑕᒻᓂᒃ ᐊᓈᓇᒻᓂᓪᓘᓃᑦ ᐃᓅᙵᕆᓕᖅᑐᓂᒃ ᐊᑦᑎᖅᓯᔭᒪᒃᐸᑕ ᖃᐅᔨᑎᑕᐅᖄᓇᐊᖅᑲᑫᔭᖅᐳᖕᓖ? ᖃᓄᖅᓕ ᐱᓇᔭᖅᐳᖕᓕ?

ᑭ. ᐱᐅᓂᖅᓴᐅᒐᓗᐊᖅᐳᖅ ᐃᓐᓇᓕᔭᐅᔪᖅ ᐊᐱᓕᔭᐅᒃᐸᑦ ᖃᐅᔨᒪᑦᑎᐊᖅᒪᑕ

ᐱᖅᑯᓯᕕᓂᑉᑎᓐᓂᒃ ᒪᓕᒃᑕᐅᕙᓚᐅᖅᑐᓂᒃ. ᒪᒃᑯᒃᑐᑦ ᑕᐃᑉᓱᒪᓂ ᐊᑦᑎᓂᒃᐸᓚᐅᖏᒪᑕ, ᐃᓐᓇᐅᓂᖅᓴᐃᑦ ᐱᓕᕆᐊᕆᓚᐅᒪᔾᔪᒃ. ᐅᐸᒥᐅᓕᖅᑐᖅ ᒪᒃᑯᒃᑐᑦ ᑭᑐᒥᐊᓂᒃ ᐊᑦᑎᖅᓯᑦᑕᓕᖅᒪᑕ ᐱᖅᑲᓐᓈᕋᓗᖕᒥᓐᓂᒃ ᐱᓯᐊᒐᒥᐊᒥᓐᓂᒃ.

ᐃᓚᖏᐊᓪᓚᑦ ᐃᖕᒥᓐᓂᒃ ᐊᑎᖅᐸᓕᖅᒪᑕ. ᑕᐃᒪ ᖃᒪᓂ'ᔭᐊᕐᒥᐅᑕᖅ ᐸᓂᖅᑲᕐᒪᑦ ᐊᕝᕙᕐᒥᓂᒃ. ᑕᐃᒪᓐᓇᐅᖏᑦᑑᒐᓗᐊᖅ.

ᐊ. ᐊᑦᑎᖅᓯᕆᐊᖃᖏᑉᐳᖓ ᓄᑕᕋᒻᓂᒃ ᐃᓅᔪᓐᓇᐃᓰᖅᑐᒥᒃ? ᐊᑎᐊ ᐊᑐᓇᐊᑲᓗᐊᖅᐸᑦ ᐃᓅᔪᓇᐃᓰᓗᐊᖅᑎᑦᑐᒍ ᓈᒪᖏᐹ?

ᑭ. ᑕᐃᑉᓱᒪᓂ ᐃᓅᔪᓐᓇᐃᓰᖅᑐᒥᒃ ᐊᑦᑎᖅᓯᖅᑯᔭᐅᓚᐅᖏᓇᑉᑕ. ᐅᐸᒥᐅᓕᖅ ᑕᐃᒪᓐᓇᐃᖏᓕᕐᒥᔭᖅ ᑭᑐᓗᒃᑖᓂᒃ ᐊᑦᑎᖅᓯᑦᑕᓕᖅᒪᑕ ᐃᓅᔪᓐᓇᐃᓰᖅᑐᐊᖅᐸᓇᓪᓛᑦ.

ᐊ. ᖃᒻᒦᑦᑕᐅᖅ ᐊᑎᖃᓇᐊᖃᔪᖕᒪᑕ, ᐃᓅᑉ ᐊᑎᐊᓂᒃ ᐊᑦᑎᖅᓯᔪᓐᓇᖅᐳᖔ ᖃᒻᒥᒥᒃ?

ᑭ. ᖃᐅᔨᒪᖏᑐᖓ ᖃᒻᒦᑦ ᐃᓄᖕᓂᒃ ᐊᑎᖃᔪᖕᒪᖖᒑᑖ. ᐆᒥᖕᒐ ᖃᐅᔨᒪᒐᓗᐊᖅᑐᖓ ᓯᕗᓪᓕᖅᐹᒥᓐᓂᒃ ᐊᑦᑎᖅᓯᔮᖕᒐᒥᒃ ᑕᑭᓗᐊᖅᑐᒥᒃ ᐊᑎᖃᐸᖏᒻᒪᑕ.ᐃᓚᖏ ᓇᐃᑦᑐᓐᓈᓂᒃ ᐊᑦᑎᖅᓯᔭᔭᑦ ᓯᕗᓪᓕᖅᐹᒥᓐᓂᒃ ᐃᒻᒪᖄ ᐊᔭᕐᓇᖏᓐᓂᖅᓴᐅᒻᒪᑦ.

ᐊ. ᖃᓄᖅ ᖃᐅᔨᔭᓇᖅᐳᖔ ᐃᓅᔪᓐᓇᐃᖅᓯᒪᔪᖅ ᐊᑎᖅᑖᕈᐊᖅᐸᑦ ᐅᕙᑎᓐᓂᒃ?

ᑭ. ᐃᓄᐃᑦ ᐃᓚᖏ ᐊᑎᖅᑖᕈᐊᔭᖕᒪᑕ ᐊᖕᒐᔭᖅᑳᑦᑕᐅᓇᓱᒋᔭᕐᒥᓐᓄᑦ ᓄᑕᕋᓛᕋᓛᑦ ᐃᓅᖖᒋᑎᑦᓗᒍ

ᓱᓕ. ᐃᒻᒪᖄ ᐋᓐᓂᐊᓕᕈᒥ ᐃᓅᓚᐅᕐᓂᕐᒥᓂ ᐊᑦᑎᖅᑕᐅᔪᒪᕗᒃᑐᑦ.

ᐊ. ᖁᕕᐊᓱᖕᒋᓐᓇᔭᕆᕙ ᑭᓇᑭᐊᖅ ᐊᑦᑎᖅᑕᐅᓐᓂᕈᒥ ᑖᒃᑯᓇᓂ ᐅᕙᒍᖅᑲᕈᐊᖕᒋᓪᓗᓂ?

ᑭ. ᐃᒻᒪᖄ ᐃᓄᐃᑦ ᐃᓚᖕᒋᑦ ᐅᖃᒥᐊᖃᔭᖅᑐᑦ ᐊᑦᑎᖅᑕᐅᓯᐊᖕᒋᒃᑯᒥᒃ. ᐃᓐᓇᐅᔪᖅ ᐊᑦᑎᖅᑕᐅᔪᒪᓐᓂᖕᒋᑉᐸᑦ ᐊᑦᑎᖅᑕᐅᒍᒥ ᐃᒻᒪᖄ ᐃᓅᔪᓐᓇᐃᓚᒃᓯᓐᓇᖃᔭᖅᑐᖅ, ᖃᐅᔾᒪᓇᒥᐊᕐᒪᑦᑕ ᐋᓂᐊᖃᔪᓗᐊᖅᑐᑦ ᓄᑕᖄᑦ ᐊᑦᑎᒃᑲᓂᐸᒃᑲᑉᑎᒍ.

ᐊ. ᐊᑦᑎᖅᓯᔪᓂ ᐃᓚᒋᔭᕐᒥᒃ ᐃᓅᔪᓐᓇᐃᖅᓯᒪᔪᒥᒃ ᒪᒥᑉᐹᓕᕐᓇᖅᐹ ᐊᑦᑎᖅᑕᐅᑎᓪᓗᒍ?

ᑭ. ᓇᒡᓕᒋᔭᕗᑦ ᐃᓅᔪᓐᓇᐃᖄᖕᖓᑦ ᓄᑕᖄᖅᑑᖅᑳᖕᖓᓪᓗ ᐊᑦᑎᖅᑕᐅᔭᖄᖕᖓᑦ ᖁᕕᐊᓇᖅᑐᖅ ᐃᓱᒪᓕᕐᓇᕐᒪᑦ ᐃᓚᒋᓂᐊᓕᕐᒥᒐᑉᑎᒍ ᖃᐃᓯᒪᓂᐊᓕᕐᒥᖕᒪᑦ. ᐃᓛᓂᒃᑯᑦ ᐊᑦᑎᖅᑕᐅᓇᖀᓗᐊᓕᖄᖕᖓᑕ ᐳᐃᒍᕐᓂᖅ ᐊᔪᕐᓇᖅᐸᖕᒪᑕ ᑭᓯᐊᓂ ᐊᑦᑎᑕᐅᔭᖄᖕᖓᑕ ᒪᒥᑉᐹᓕᕐᓇᖅᑐᖅ.

ᐊ. ᖃᓄᕐᓕ ᐊᑦᑎᖅᓯᓂᖅ ᐅᑎᖅᑎᑦᑎᔪᓐᓇᖅᐸ ᑕᐃᑉᓱᒥᖕᖓ ᐃᓅᙵᕆᓕᖅᑐᒥᒃ?

ᑭ. ᐃᙳᑕᕗᑦ ᐊᑎᖅᑲᕐᒪᑕ ᐃᓚᕆᓚᐅᖅᑕᑉᑎᓐᓂᒃ ᐅᐃᓚᐅᕋᓗ, ᐊᖕᒐᔪᖅᑳᑎᓚᐅᖅᑕᑉᑎᓐᓂᒡᒎᓐᓃᑦ ᓱᕗᓕᕕᓂᑉᑎᓐᓂᒃ. ᐊᑖᑕᒪᓗ ᐅᐃᕆᓚᐅᖅᑕᕐᒪᓗ ᐊᑖᑖᑕ ᓄᑕᕋᕗᑦ ᐊᑦᑎᖅᑐᓚᐅᕐᒪᕆᑦ, ᑎᐊ'ᓇ ᐱᓱᓚᐅᕐᒪᑕ.

Tuq&urausiit

ᑐᖅᖢᕋᐅᓰᑦ

Inuit Kinship and Naming Customs

Edited by
Pelagie Owlijoot and
Louise Flaherty

Translated by
Pelagie Owlijoot

Published by Inhabit Media Inc.
www.inhabitmedia.com

Inhabit Media Inc. (Iqaluit) P.O. Box 11125, Iqaluit, Nunavut, X0A 1H0
(Toronto) 146A Orchard View Blvd., Toronto, Ontario, M4R 1C3

Cover design by Inhabit Media Inc.

We acknowledge the support of the Canada Council for the Arts for our publishing program.

Printed in Canada.

Library and Archives Canada Cataloguing in Publication

Inuit ilagiigusinggit amma attiqtuijjusinggit / aaqkiksuqtaujut Pilaji Aulajjut amma Luis Vlaahurti ; tukiliuqtaujuq Pilaji Aulajjut = Inuit kinship and naming customs / edited by Pelagie Owlijoot and Louise Flaherty ; translated by Pelagie Owlijoot.

Summary: A collection of interviews by Pelagie Owlijoot with Inuit elders from Arviat Region, Nunavut, about traditional family naming and kinship customs.
Text in Inuktitut (in syllabic characters) and English; translated from the Inuktitut; title in Inuktitut romanized.
ISBN 978-1-927095-71-3 (pbk.)

1. Inuit--Kinship--Canada. 2. Names, Inuit--Canada. 3. Inuit--Canada--Social life and customs. 4. Inuit elders--Canada--Interviews. I. Owlijoot, Pelagie, translator, interviewer (expression), editor of compilation II. Flaherty, Louise, editor of compilation III. Title: Inuit kinship and naming customs.

E99.E7I5786 2014 306.83089'9712 C2013-908438-X

CONTENTS

Introduction

Pelagie Owlijoot & Louise Flaherty

Tuq&urausiit is a term used by Inuit to address our relatives, acknowledging the relationships and kinships that bind us. Inuit use *tuq&urausiit* to show respect and foster closeness within our families. Naming keeps our family histories alive and encourages us to work together and rely on each other through hardship. *Tuq&urausiit* also helps to promote healthier communities, resulting in less crime and violence.

However, the custom of *tuq&urausiit* has quickly been disappearing. Inuit living in communities today often address each other by their English first names, rather than their traditional kinship terms. This is one of the reasons we are losing closeness in our relationships within our own families.

That is why it is crucial to record the knowledge of those few remaining Inuit elders who know the traditional kinship and naming practices. If knowledge of these practices is not recorded—soon—it will be forgotten and lost for good. The knowledge of our elders must be written down in order for it to survive and be passed on from generation to generation.

This book presents interviews with elders from Arviat, Nunavut, who were asked about *tuq&urausiit* and other kinship and naming customs in Kivalliq Region, the southernmost of the three regions of Nunavut. The importance of passing down this knowledge cannot be overstated. Knowing our roots as individuals is key to becoming successful in life.

We hope that this book helps the younger generation to preserve the custom of *tuq&urausiit*.

Pronunciation Guide

aik (ai-k): Brother-in-law to a sister-in-law, or vice versa.

amauq (a-mow-rk): Great-grandmother / grandfather.

anaana (a-naa-na): Mother.

angutiqatigiit (ango-tee-rka-tee-geet): Cousins whose fathers are brothers.

aniksaq (a-nek-sark): The term a female cousin would use to address her male cousin in South Baffin / Nunavik.

anikuluk (anee-ko-look): Brother.

arnaqatigiit (ar-na-rka-tee-geet): Cousins whose mothers are sisters.

arnarvik (are-nar-vek): Mother's sister (aunt) in Amitturmiut/Kivalliq.

ataata (a-taa-ta): Father.

atsiaq (at-seeark): The one named after.

avvaq (ab-baq): A term used for two people named after the same person. Dual form: **avvariik.**

qaplunaaq (krab-low-nark): A term used for a non-Inuk; white person.

sauniriit (sow-ne-reet): The person who receives a name; what Prince George is to King George.

tuq&uraq (turk-thlo-rark): To address someone by a kinship term.

tuq&urarniq (turk-thlo-raw-nerk) or **tuq&urausiq** (turk-thlo-row-sirk): The practice of kinship. Plural form: **tuq&urarniit** or **tuq&urausiit**.

Chapter One

The Custom of Naming

James Konek

Interview Date

June 2012

Q. What can you tell me about the custom of naming?

A. When naming a newborn, you don't choose from random names. The people you name your baby after are your elders

first—your grandparents or parents. Today, people are naming their children after anyone they like. That is one of the reasons why newborns die at an early age, because their parents are naming them after people they do not even know. Our custom was to name children after our family members. Young Inuit today do not have a lot of knowledge, but act like they know everything. That is really different from how we were back then.

Q. What about naming a child—would this child carry the *tuq&urausiq* of his or her namesake?

A. Young people should not be giving their children random names. Elders from Baker Lake, Rankin Inlet, and Arviat have a lot of knowledge about who they are related to. Our grandparents know who we are related to and can help us name our relatives. People are just gathering a lot of the same information and passing it around in the education system. They are giving names to children that they shouldn't, because they are not the names of relatives. It is our custom to name children after our relatives.

Leo Sr. Ahmak

Interview Date

July 2012

Q. Have you ever named children? What can you tell me about the custom of naming?

A. Our children today are all named after our elders of my generation.

Q. What about naming a child—would this child carry the *tuq&urausiq* of his or her namesake?

A. Yes, there are some people who carry the *tuq&urausiit* that their namesakes used, but there are others who use their own nicknames, because we love our children very much. Some of them tend to have nicknames that their parents give out of love. Some parents tend to love a child who is named after their in-laws more than a child who is named after their parents. It was our custom to follow that.

Q. What effects does it have to give children special treatment because of their namesakes?

A. That is how some people are when a child is named after someone they respected; they usually give the parents special treatment. Some people use nicknames and other people start to call them by that, too, but there are others who use their real

names. Inuit dialects are different in each community, so some use shorter names.

Q. Does having and naming children reflect your standing in the community?

A. Yes, we have raised quite a few children. We have adopted children and we also have our own biological children. These are signs that we are respected, and it has good effects on our lives. People give children to those they think will be good parents, so when we were given a child, it was out of respect.

Q. When a child is named after someone deceased, can it help calm the family and ease the pain of having lost a loved one?

A. Yes, it helps to ease the pain of having lost a loved one, and it also makes you happier. The agony and grieving cease a lot sooner once you have the name back in your family. Some people even say, "I'm lucky I have him or her back, because I really loved him or her." That's what some Inuit say, when they name a family member after someone who is deceased.

Q. Have you noticed any changes where *tuq&urausiit* are concerned?

A. No, as far as I can remember, I have not noticed any changes in *tuq&urausiit*, because we have used them for years. I have not seen any changes in *tuq&urausiit* with other Inuit either.

Q. How important was the naming of a child?

A. It is very important, because it's a way of helping us recognize who our relatives are. It helps us to know the people around us through names, so it is important to name children after our relatives.

Q. In those days, were naming and *tuq&urarniq* more common than they are today?

A. Yes; in the past we just used our Inuktitut name that was given to us at birth. It is still common today for some people just to address them by their Inuktitut given names, or, if we are related to them, to *tuq&uraq* them.

Q. Does the naming process have an effect on the namesake?

A. Yes, when a child is named after an elder and the elder says something to his or her namesake when the baby is born, it affects the child because the elder's words are so strong. These things really happen. Even if the child did not understand as a newborn, these effects start happening in the child's life.

Q. Did *tuq&urausiit* vary for people on an individual basis?

A. Yes, *tuq&urausiit* are different based on the region or community you live in. I'm from Arviat, and when I compare my

tuq&urausiq with other communities, there are differences, because of our dialects.

Matilda Sulurayok

Interview Date

July 2012

Q. What can you tell me about the custom of naming?

A. My oldest children were all named by my mother. When my mother passed away, I started naming my grandchildren and my two youngest children. My mother named my oldest child Tuutaa, and his nickname is Aapai. The person she named him after was my brother-in-law, who drowned. He was a young adult when he went swimming with three other guys and died from drowning.

I only have four children of my own. When I had Rosie, I called my mother soon after she was born. My mother asked me, "If you have a girl, who do you think should be her name?" I said, "It's a girl, so I do not want her to go hunting for food or work too hard, so I want to name her after my father. What do you think about that?" Her response was, "Yes, it's okay." Now my daughter is named after my father, Issakiark. I really wanted to name my father as a girl, so he could rest from all the hard work he did for my family. Back then he literally had nothing—no hunting equipment when we were living on the land. The men used to hunt by dog teams, and sometimes by foot, for many miles. I could not stop thinking about how hard my father had worked for us to survive, so I wanted to name him as my daughter. So I did.

Judy was born when Rosie was three years old. Judy was named by my mother-in-law. My mother-in-law's name was

Ujaralaaq, and she was Naujaq's wife. Judy's name is Siulluk, after my mother-in-law's brother-in-law. Of all the children I have had, I have only named Rosie and Judy myself. I have three children, Rosie and Judy and my son, and the fourth was my youngest, but he was adopted by a couple in Rankin Inlet, now living in Whale Cove. The Ussaks adopted our youngest son.

He was only the second son I had, and I really did not want to give him away. I gave him up for adoption because our parents made the final decision about our children. They taught us so many things related to life and childrearing. My oldest son does not have a brother, so I did not want to give away my second son to be adopted, but my mother said she wanted him to be adopted so I had no choice. That's what the elders before us did, so we obeyed what they said.

Q. What about naming a child—would this child carry the *tuq&urausiq* of his or her namesake?

A. Yes, children used to carry the *tuq&urausiit* of their namesakes in the past. Today we are not using *tuq&urausiit* as much as we did, including me. I tell my children, "You will have to pass on what I taught you, so remember the things I tell you."

Q. What effects does it have to give children special treatment because of their namesake?

A. Yes, naming has a big effect, depending on the relationship of the person you named. I became more serious since I started

naming infants, and as I got older, too. When naming someone you respect, you get a sense of being useful as an elder. My grandson, Rosie's son, is named after me; he's living in Rankin Inlet right now.

Ivan is named after me because my daughter asked if she could name him after me, and I said she could. She named him Ivan because he's a boy and will be able to do a lot of things that I couldn't do, like speak and understand English. He is going to do things for me now. I was in Winnipeg when Rosie called me to ask if she could name Ivan after me.

Q. Were you respected for your namesake, perhaps by someone that was not closely related to you?

A. Yes, I was respected by some elders when I was up in Rankin Inlet because of my name. I have been told by a few people, "Your namesake is a hard worker who got his job done, even when his parents were not around." I wasn't too impressed, because they said he is better than I am. He is able to speak English and can work at higher-paying jobs.

I visited my brother-in-law and he told me I have a good namesake. I asked him who my namesake was, and he said, "Kimaliarjuk." I asked him, "Where is he from?" He responded, "The guy who works at the airport." I remembered and said to him jokingly, "I am not impressed that he is better than me."

Q. When a child is named after the deceased, can it help calm the family of the deceased and ease the pain of having lost a loved one?

A. Yes, it helps to ease the pain a lot, and the healing process seems to speed up. When one of your parents or your relatives has been named by anyone, even if it's not someone closely related, it helps to ease the pain a lot. I am really thankful that my mother has been named in Rankin Inlet by her cousins there.

I was really lifted emotionally and my conscience seemed to become clearer. I had a sense of peace, and also appreciation and gratitude somehow, when I heard my mother was named. For me, naming is a serious thing, and it is our tradition, and we should continue, as it is important.

Q. Have you noticed changes where *tuq&urausiit* are concerned?

A. Yes, it has changed a lot, because in the past we were told to use *tuq&urausiit* to all our relatives. My father and his younger brother were the only two children in their family, and they both had children. My father's younger brother had two sons and two daughters. The women, my cousins, I call them *angutiqatiit*, and both his sons, who have passed away, I would have called my *aniksaqs*, because they were my *akkak*'s [paternal uncle's] children.

My brother Innosar, who I *tuq&uraq anikuluk*, and also my uncle's sons, I use the same *tuq&urausiq* to them: *anikuluk*. We were serious about using *tuq&urausiit* at that time.

Q. How important was the naming of a child?

A. I learned from my grandmother. She taught me a lot of things regarding life for the future. One of the things she taught me is to plan ahead of time before taking action. Naming is something you have to be careful with; you have to get confirmation from an elder first before naming someone. This was always a rule used in the past. The reason I started naming my children myself is because I am now the oldest person left in my family. My brother Paul is our youngest. There are only three of us left: me, Simona, and Paul.

My daughter Rosie often asks me who she should name when she has a child. I once told her that a lot of things have changed, including Inuit lifestyles.

Young people are not contacting or notifying their parents when they have a baby, so often the grandparents don't know the gender of the baby for some time. That's not right, but what can you do? Naming is still very important today, and we still have to follow our traditions. If we want to name an elder, maybe a father-in-law or mother-in-law, we still do that. The elders of the family should decide who the child will be named after. It was always like that, and I still tend to use that rule of naming.

Q. In those days, were naming and *tuq&urarniq* more common than they are today?

A. Yes, we did use *tuq&urausiit* a lot more than we are using them today. Even I was using it all the time to all my relatives in the past. Once we found out who we were related to, we were told, "You are related to him or her, so he or she is your 'aunt' or

'uncle.'" Today, elders included, it does not seem to matter anymore, since we lost too much already. Most young people are speaking English too much.

Q. Did *tuq&urausiit* vary for people on an individual basis?

A. Yes, it has always been like that where we come from. I have always lived in the Kivalliq region. My mother was from the Arviat area, and my father was from Ukkusiksalik, farther up north. My father lived with my grandmother until she got really old. My grandmother taught us a lot about *tuq&urausiit,* how to treat your husband, how to raise children, and how to sew men's clothing fit for winter and summer. There were a lot of things she taught us.

Since we started living in communities and modern houses, we are not teaching our children what was taught to us. Even elders that have been taught these things and know them very well are not sharing or teaching them to their children. We have all gone through drastic changes within our culture, so trying to cope with change and new lifestyles has affected all of us. Part of it is good, but it is hard on the older people.

Nancy Tasseor

Interview Date

August 2012

Q. What can you tell me about the custom of naming?

A. My relatives are my daughters, my sons, my mother-in-law, and my father-in-law. I *tuq&uraq* my child named after my father *atchiaq*. That is how my parents taught me, so I use *tuq&urausiit* that I have learned from my parents. As a family, we *tuq&uraq* each other rather than using names. Some families call a child named after their mother *anaana* or a child named after their father as *ataata*. That is how it is today. When a sister or cousin gets married, we *tuq&uraq* her husband our *aik*, and vice versa. We do not use their names, as it is impolite and shameful if we use our *aik*'s names; we should not even talk to them, as it is our custom to show respect.

Q. What about naming a child—would this child carry the *tuq&urausiq* of his or her namesake?

A. We call our namesakes *abbaq*. Inuit called it *abbariik*, meaning people who have the same name. Our children are named after elders; I myself even have a namesake, whom I call *abbaq*. I have a lot of namesakes everywhere now. When they are named after us, we still call them *abbaq* when we have the same names.

Q. When a child is named after the deceased, can it help the family of the deceased by calming them and helping to ease the pain of having lost a loved one?

A. Yes, when naming someone who has passed away, Inuit wait a while to name the person. When you name a child after a deceased person, yes, it does calm you down, and you feel so much better emotionally and mentally. Even if it is just a baby that was named after someone who passed away, it makes you feel so much better.

Q. Have you noticed any changes where the *tuq&urausiit* are concerned?

A. Yes, I'm starting to hear these new *tuq&urausiit* that I think are coming from other communities. The ones that we did not hear very often before are being used today. Another concern I have is not pronouncing their whole names. Some Inuit are now calling each other through short-form names. For example, Kaunuaq, we call him Kaun for short. I think the adults are just copying what their youth are saying.

Q. How important was the naming of a child?

A. Not too long ago, Inuit used only Inuktitut names, but I think they started calling each other by English names when the missionaries started giving children English names after blessing them. There are some people whose Inuktitut names I do not even know now.

Q. In those days, were naming and *tuq&urarniq* more common than they are today?

A. Yes, they were. Back then we used to talk only in Inuktitut, so *tuq&urausiit* were common. Our relationships were better, too, because we were like one big family. Today we do not know who we are related to anymore, because we use names rather then *tuq&urausiit*.

Q. Did *tuq&urausiit* vary for people on an individual basis?

A. Yes, I am not used to hearing other people's ways of *tuq&uraniq*. I do not understand some of them. The first time I hear another region's *tuq&urausiit*, they are difficult to understand. Even when I listen to their conversations, I still do not understand how they are related. In Arviat, relatives used *tuq&urausiit*. Cousins or friends used their Inuktitut names.

ᑐᖅᑲ ᓗᕋᐅᓰᑦ

Chapter Two

Usefulness and Importance of *Tuq&urausiit*

Leo Sr. Ahmak

Interview Date
July 2012

Q. Have you heard about *sauniriit* [great-grandchildren], and how was that term used?

A. Yes, I have heard about *sauniriit*, and *amauq* [great-grandfather or -grandmother]. I am a true Inuk, so I know about these things that my ancestors used. *Sauniq* is my grandchild's child, and they would call me *amauq*.

Q. Are *tuq&urausiit* gender-specific?

A. Yes, there are differences. Men and women have their own *tuq&urausiit*. There are a lot of differences, and it makes sense.

Q. What names were you given, and how many names do you have?

A. My name is Ahmaq, and it was given to me at birth; it has always been my name. Then I was named Leo by the missionaries, and when the Ahiarmiut were relocated to our community, a man named Kaajak, who I think loved me, asked me, "What's your name?" I said, "Ahmaq." His response was "Eehh, Ahmanaaq," and since that time, I've been Ahmanaaq.

Q. Have you ever seen or heard about individuals who did not want a name in a certain household, or wanted a name in a certain household?

A. When you want to name a child after someone who is not related to you, you always have to get permission first from their elder. What usually happens is that if an elder wants to be named in a certain family, they will ask in advance.

Q. Have you heard of a case where there is no name to give a newborn?

A. I know that when a young woman has a baby, the parents usually give them an English name and their parents or grandparents name the child in Inuktitut. Maybe because they don't know their family too well, or because it has always been our tradition for our elders to do the naming.

Q. Were there cases of a child already having a name picked out even before he or she was born?

A. Some people pick a name for children even before they are born. Usually how it happens is if you repeatedly dream about a deceased person, it means that they want to be named. When the deceased wants to be named to a certain family, they are named through dreams.

Q. When you were growing up, were you taught about your names?

A. I was not taught about my name, but I knew that we were named after our grandparents or other relatives. My mother named me after her brother-in-law, Ahmaq. That's the name my mother gave me, so this name continued on in my family line.

Q. Do you think that sometimes people seek guidance or help from their namesakes?

A. Some Inuit elders were brought up to understand that if we truly love our namesakes or our children, we have to teach and train them to work hard as they are growing up. It is easier to grow up working hard because we tend to get into trouble as young people when we get bored. If we want our namesakes to have a good, productive life, they should be put to work as soon as they are able to handle it.

Q. Were there cases when parents did not have any sons, and would consequently treat their daughter as if she were their son?

A. Yes, when parents have only girls and do not have boys, they would have them do boys' chores. One example is picking up cache meat by dog team, and other things that men usually do.

Q. Is it important to keep our children informed about our relatives?

A. Yes, today it's important to keep our children informed about how to *tuq&uraq* our relatives, as well as older people. Sometimes we don't realize who we are related to, even though they have been with us for a while or even all our lives. I think it's important that we understand who we are related to and also how to *tuq&uraq* each other.

Q. Do *tuq&urausiit* serve the purpose of bringing people closer together? Is it truly unique to Inuit?

A. I'm going to tell you something important and true. I have many relatives, and we have different ways of using *tuq&urausiit* for individuals. When I know that I am related to someone, I use the *tuq&urausiq* that was used for that namesake. This relationship with my relatives has helped bring us closer together. It helps make me less afraid or hesitant to ask for anything from my relatives—I can just be openly friendly and ask questions if I don't know, without being embarrassed about life issues. It helps keep our relatives close, because it brings us closer together.

Q. When the first white people started to settle, be they missionaries or traders, did they also recognize *tuq&urausiit* of certain individuals?

A. I remember when the traders first arrived and the stores first started opening in Arviat. Our fathers and other men would bring hides and fox pelts to the store, and they would write their names down. Also, missionaries used to travel to camps during the summer or winter and visit for a while. They would communicate with our parents and grandparents and learn from them.

Matilda Sulurayok

Interview Date

July 2012

Q. How were *tuq&urausiit* useful?

A. They were and still are very useful today. I remember my grandfather, who is my step-grandfather, who taught us. My mother was adopted and she had some stepsisters and step-brothers, and I *tuq&uraq* all of them. It is a different dialect from Arviat's *tuq&urausiq* because we lived somewhere else when I was growing up. I call them my *arnarviks* [aunts] and my *aniksaqs* [uncles]. I still use these *tuq&urausiit* when I address them up to today because they are living in Rankin Inlet. There are only two of them left.

Q. Have you heard about *sauniriit* [great-grandchildren]?

A. Yes, I have; I even have *sauniriit*. They are my grandchildren's children.

Q. I suppose what I am trying to understand is, in *tuq&urausiit*, how was that term used?

A. *Sauniq* has a few meanings, depending on where you come from. I think Arviat became a community before Rankin Inlet. Chesterfield Inlet, Repulse Bay, and Coral Harbour use almost

the same *tuq&urausiit*.

When my grandchild has a baby, that's when I call that child *sauniq*. That's how it was in the past.

Q. Are *tuq&urausiit* gender-specific?

A. Yes, there are many differences. A woman cannot say *ujuruk* [a term used by a woman's brother for his nieces and nephews]. I cannot say that to my brother's children. I would call my brother's children *irngutaq* [grandchildren], based on what women have always used. My grandmother was from Ukkusiksalik, so I had learned these from her and still use them today.

Q. What names were you given and how many names do you have?

A. I have only one name. I had two older sisters who passed away before I was born. An old Ahiarmiut man from the Baker Lake area, who is not related to us, visited my parents in Chesterfield Inlet when they were there for Christmas, and he requested to be named.

When I was growing up as a child in Chesterfield Inlet, I remember seeing him visiting my parents. The old man did not know my mother was pregnant, but he had said to my father, "Name your next child after me, so the child will have a long, productive life." So that's how I got my name, Kimaliarjuk. I never really liked him, because he was an old man with a very bad voice, and he died when he was really old.

Q. Have you ever seen or heard about individuals who did not want a name in a certain household, or who wanted a name in a certain household?

A. No, I have not heard about that before. The story I told you about the old man who I am named after is a good example. Even though he came from a different family and from a different community, he asked my parents if he could be named. My grandmother also agreed on having his name in my family, because he said I will live a long time and have a good life. Elders were the decision-makers for anything to do with life.

When a child is named after you, you would take the infant when you saw him or her for the first time and speak to the child—more like a promise about how good her or his life will be. That's the way it was, and I still believe it exists today for some Inuit. Sometimes I wonder how the young people today name their children themselves, even though they are young.

In the past, elders or parents did the naming when someone in the family had a child. It has really changed a lot, and as elders today, we know it's happening, but what can you do? I'm sure I'm not the only elder who is concerned about it.

Q. Have you ever heard of a case where there is no name to give a newborn?

A. I know that it happens today that a child comes home without a name. Today Inuit seem to have problems naming their children, because they are confused. Elders are not teaching their children these things, and we have abandoned our responsibil-

ity. Some young people probably know this and have been taught, like most of us were.

I feel sorry for our young Inuit today because they have not been taught important issues and our traditions regarding naming children. It's obvious that they are not sure who to ask when they have a child. In the past we lived in camps, so it was not complicated like it is today.

Q. Were there any cases of a child already having a name picked out before he or she was even born?

A. Yes, some of us were already named before we were born. I already had a name before I was born because the old man I was talking about wanted the next child in the family to be named after him. My two older sisters had not lived very long, and this old man came to my family and said, "She'll live a longer life, so I want her to have my name," when I was still in my mother's womb.

Q. When you were growing up, were you taught about your names?

A. When I was growing up, I knew I had been named after an elder. I have only one name and I saw my namesake once in a while when I was growing up, a very tall, old man. I didn't really like him, but I couldn't do anything about it because my name cannot be changed. He said a lot of things to me and he was ugly, so I didn't really like him.

Q. Do you think that sometimes people seek guidance or help from their namesakes?

A. The only people that were in control of naming were the elders of the camps at the time. My grandmother was always talking or making decisions based on the future. She told me not to pick random names when I start having children, and when Tikiq [my cousin] started having children, my grandmother told him the same thing. She said naming is serious and that it is attached to human nature, and something that is not to be taken lightly. She told us to be considerate when we start naming our children, and if we are not asked by an elder, not to name other family members. She told us that our lives were already planned even before we were born, so if we want to name a non-family member, we should always ask the elders of the family first. It is important that they know and agree, and then we can name a child after someone other than a family member. That's the way it was in the past.

Q. If there are cases when a boy is named after a woman, would he have to be dressed like a girl? How exactly does that work?

A. Not that I know of. Like my brother was named Niaqurluk, after my grandmother, and Innosar when he got baptized. His Inuktitut name is Niaqurluk, and even though he's a boy, he is named after my grandmother because she wanted to be named through a boy. It seemed like when a woman was pregnant, elders knew if it was a boy or a girl, even before the baby was born.

My grandmother knew the baby was a boy, so she wanted

to be named through him. That's why my brother's name is Innosar. Elders today, like me, often don't know the gender of an unborn child, but our elders before us knew so much about life.

Q. Were there cases when parents did not have any sons, and would consequently treat their daughter as if she were their son?

A. Yes, that did happen often in the past. My brothers Innosar and Paul were the only boys in our family, with five women. There used to be five of us sisters. My mother obviously raised us, and my late younger sister Celina was able to do a lot of things that men do, because my mother taught her to be tough. She was able to hunt on her own, and when she caught a caribou she was able to skin it as well, just like a man.

So yes, this always happened in the past. The little boys would do the same as well, when there were no sewing machines. When we did our sewing by hand, the boys would do the same, like making mitts for themselves. Men used to go out hunting every day when they became adults. Some were also trained to sew clothes, so they would be able to mend their own hunting clothing when they were away hunting for a long time.

My father and my uncle were great hunters, and my uncle was able to sew everything himself because my grandmother taught him how to do it. Our grandmother taught him to work hard. When my father and my uncle were out hunting for a long time, he was able to sew caribou parkas and socks out of fresh caribou skins. My uncle was able to do a lot of things on his own.

Q. Is it important that we keep our children informed about our relatives?

A. Yes, it is. I often tell my children and grandchildren who we are related to and how they should use *tuq&urausiit*, but it is harder to use them nowadays. Nobody uses *tuq&urausiit* now because everyone calls each other by their English names. Back then, when we were growing up, we used only *tuq&urausiit*. I tell my children who our relatives are and tell them to get to know each other better so they will get closer to each other.

Q. Do *tuq&urausiit* serve the purpose of bringing people closer together?

A. Yes, it brought us Inuit a lot closer together when we used them every day. Inuit who were related also helped each other with everything. If someone needed help with something, we were ready anytime to lend a hand, but today, since we are living in houses now, we do not even visit our relatives anymore. Inuit families also worked together when there were big projects to do, like skinning caribou and seals if many were caught. We are not like that anymore; we have stopped helping each other. That is one of the big changes that has happened, and I think about it often.

Q. When the first white people started to settle, be they missionaries or traders, did they also recognize your *tuq&urausiit* to certain individuals?

A. I do not think so; they did not recognize our *tuq&urausiit* because Inuit were scared of white people at that time. In Chesterfield Inlet I saw *qublunaaq* [white] RCMP officers, traders, priests, nuns, and radio operators; they were the only *qublunaat* in the community.

Nancy Tasseor

Interview Date
August 2012

Q. Have you heard about *sauniriit* [great-grandchildren]?

A. No, I do not know how this term is used. I have not heard about this *tuq&urausiq*. Perhaps it's the people from farther up north who use it. I still do not understand some of them.

Q. Are *tuq&urausiit* gender-specific?

A. Yes, for cousins *arnaqatigiit* [cousins whose mothers are sisters] or *angutiqatigiit* [cousins whose fathers are brothers] is our dialect. I understand these *tuq&urausiit*, but I do not hear Inuit use them as often now. There are some of us who still call each other by *tuq&urausiit*, like me and my cousins. Calling each other "mother-in-law" or "father-in-law" is in the past. Today I do not hear too many *tuq&urausiit* being used.

Q. Were names used to regulate dating?

A. I do not know if names were used to regulate dating. Our parents were responsible for choosing who their children were going to marry. The young people had no choice, because parents made the decisions. Sometimes we did not even know who was going to marry who.

Q. What names were you given, and how many names do you have?

A. My parents named me Kablutsiak, and it has always been my name. Inuit do not often call me by other names. After my blessings from the missionaries, Inuit started calling me Nancy, and sometimes they use my Inuktitut name.

Q. Has the way parents choose names for their children changed?

A. Yes, I think when the Inuit women give birth down south, some younger mothers do not name their newborns. Some may name a friend they like after talking with each other. Inuit are starting to name their children after someone they like from other places; some even have more than one name now. The generations before me did not have many names.

Q. Did parents get to choose the names for their children themselves?

A. Our parents or in-laws used to name our children, and younger people had no control over naming our children.

Q. Were there any cases of a child already having a name picked out even before he or she was born?

A. Yes, there are some that are named even before they are born. When the child is born, he or she would own the name and have their own *tuq&urausiit*.

Q. When you were growing up, were you taught about your names?

A. No, I was not taught about my name; my mother named me and called me by my Inuktitut name as I was growing up.

Q. Do you think that sometimes people seek guidance or help from their namesakes?

A. Yes, when we get a namesake we always want what is best for them. Some Inuit already knew the practice of Christianity, and so English names are common and used more.

Q. If a boy was given a woman's name, would he act like a girl, and vice versa?

A. Some children will play with any toy as they are growing up, whether it is for boys or girls. My mother taught me as I was growing up, so I did what she did.

The little boys spent their time outside with their fathers, learning how to run dog teams and building *igluit*, just doing things that boys do.

Q. So boys learned from their fathers, and girls learned from their mothers?

A. Our parents taught us the things that applied to us when we were growing up. Our fathers taught the boys, and they learned by observing and doing hands-on activities, like helping their father as they make *qamutiks* and learning how they are used. Some children probably had no problem understanding the lifestyles of both men and women.

Q. Do *tuq&urausiit* serve the purpose of bringing people closer together? Are they unique to Inuit?

A. Yes, when we tell children about who they are related to and their *tuq&urausiit*, they start to feel more welcome. They stop questioning and start to feel very close to being relatives with some families after finding out who they are related to. The ones that listen to older people tend to know a little better about who they are related to.

Q. When the first white people started to settle, be they missionaries or traders, did they also recognize your *tuq&urausiit* to certain individuals?

A. Some *qablunaat* [white people] who were taught by Inuit understood. Inuit and white people did not understand each other at first, but they started to understand each other after a while. Maybe some missionaries understood, because they

helped name the children of Inuit in English. Perhaps some of them remember.

Chapter Three

How *Tuq&urausiit* Was Done

Leo Sr. Ahmak

Interview Date

July 2012

Q. Is it better to wait a while after someone has passed away to name a child after him or her?

A. Our ancestors were wise and took their time in everything; they didn't rush to do important things in life. If someone passed away, we were told not to name a child after them right away, but to wait at least a year. We also must get permission before naming a non-relative.

Q. Could anyone do the naming, or was it the responsibility of an elder?

A. If our grandparents were alive, they knew who we were related to and they could tell us who we should name. So a woman who has just had a child should seek advice from an elder who knows. That's how naming should be done.

Q. What about naming dogs? Of course, dogs need names. I suppose they do not get named after humans?

A. You can name your dogs any names you like. If I had three to six dogs I would give them all a name, human or any name. They will eventually start to understand their names.

Q. How can I tell when a deceased person wishes to have a name in my family?

A. As couples, we need to communicate about everything, so we agree on a name for a child. If you want to name someone who is deceased, go see their relatives or the elder of the family.

Don't call them on the phone—see them in person so you can talk better and agree upon it.

Q. How does the deceased choose which family to pass his or her name on to? Is it based on if they were friends of the family or anything else?

A. Before the arrival of the missionaries and the Canadian government, Inuit have always been naming. If you are friends with the deceased person you want to name, you won't hesitate to ask the family. They will agree with no hesitation if you want to name your friend.

Q. Can the opposite also happen? Can an individual be displeased because he or she does not want his or her name placed in a family?

A. As long as you ask, most Inuit will agree to be named. As Inuit, we hold on to love tightly, and we feel it, too. Most of us are caring and sensitive to others, so most times Inuit will agree to be named, as long as the family agrees.

Q. Can you interpret the practice of naming as a form of reincarnation?

A. Inuit men usually are not the ones naming; we know it as a woman's responsibility. When our wives or our children

want to name someone, they ask the elder or a relative who is older than us. They name their children after what the elder wants them to name the child. I believe that reincarnation happens when someone is named. We love our family and friends very much and watch every move they make, making sure they are okay.

Matilda Sulurayok

Interview Date
July 2012

Q. So when a newborn was named after a lost relative, would the infant be treated as if the infant were actually his or her namesake?

A. Yes, the generations before me treated the infant the same as they did the namesake. My namesake, who was an old man, came to see me shortly after I was born and said that I would be able to do many things and be able to work on sealskins skilfully, because they are really useful for men and children. When there were no houses, animal skins were really important. He said to me that I would be able to work on animal skins professionally, but I do not remember him telling me this because I was a newborn.

As I grew older, my mother and my grandmother used to make sealskin tents, and during the winter they used caribou skin tents and sometimes lived in *igluit*. I used to watch my mother and my grandmother working on skins and constantly preparing meats for the family, drying caribou meat and fish and preparing the meat as it became available. I watched them and learned from them.

When I got older I wanted to be like my grandmother, aunts, and mother, working on sealskins and caribou skins. When I watched them handling skins, using only their *uluit*, it looked really easy to do. It looked so fun and easy, so I started thinking that I would be like them when I got older.

One time I told my grandmother that I wanted to learn

to work with skins, like her. She told me to cut off seal flippers, so I did. She told me to pull off the skin and said, "That's the way you'll learn to work with skins." I kept practicing with those little flippers, trying to clean them as much as I could. They made us practice with a lot of things. They did not worry about how tired or bored we were as soon as we were able to work.

Q. Could anyone do the naming, or was it the responsibility of an elder?

A. Today, anybody names whoever they like, so we are in the middle of tough times. In the past, Inuit used to name their children only after family members, or people they appreciated and were thankful to. Someone who had been very helpful to a family was given a name within that family. This has changed a lot, and elders can see these changes occurring.

We were told that it is not right to name a child after someone you had just met or to just choose a name that you like, and that is exactly what is happening today. As young people, we were in no way responsible for naming our own children ourselves. It was impossible—not the right thing to do. My mother and my mother-in-law were the only ones who named my children.

Q. What happens when someone outside the immediate family of the deceased is named after them? For instance, if my father or mother passed away and someone who is not related to me

named their child after my mother or father, is it important that I be notified? And how do I react?

A. Yes, it's important to be notified by someone who is not a relative if they want to name a child after your parents. If I don't want them to be named, they should not be named. Yes and no are very important words when naming someone.

For me, when someone asks me, I get kind of excited and happy. When someone wants to name a family member, you become emotional and thankful. My late husband Sulurayok wanted to be named by someone he is related to in Coral Harbour. I was really thankful that time, because he had passed away a year earlier. When I was asked if they could name him I could not refuse, because they were related to Sulurayok on his mother's side. It is a good feeling, both mentally and emotionally.

Q. Is it discouraged to name a child after someone who has recently died? That is, to use a person's name so soon after their death?

A. Yes, it was really important to wait at least a year to name someone who had recently died. Today we do not follow that tradition anymore, and we do not teach our young people anymore.

Q. What about naming dogs? Of course, dogs need names. I suppose they do not get named after humans?

A. My father never named his dogs after human beings, and I do

not know of anybody naming a dog after a human. In those days, dogs were our only transportation and they were put hard to work, so it was not right to name a dog after a human being. Perhaps there are some people who cannot bear children that would name dogs after their parents. I don't know.

Q. How can I tell when the deceased wishes to have a name in my family?

A. It is usually best to notify the family first if you want to name one of their deceased relatives. Ask the elder of the family, and if they agree, then you can name the person.

Q. How does the deceased choose which family to pass on his or her name to? Is it based on if they were friends of the family, or anything else?

A. My mother told me before she passed away that she does not want to be named by too many people who are not related to us. She only wanted to be named by people she knew well.

My grandmother told my mother that when she starts having children and someone she is not related to asks to be named in our family, that she should agree, especially if they are elders, because they are being honest about wanting to be named.

Q. Can the opposite also happen? Can an individual be displeased because he or she does not want his or her name placed in a family?

A. Yes, it can also happen like that too. There were some people who did not want to be named at all, because they wanted to be left alone. So nobody would name them because they didn't want to be named, even in their own family.

Q. Does naming a child after someone who has passed away help ease the pain of losing a loved one?

A. Yes, you get the person back to life through naming. When you have a grandchild named after someone you loved or a family member or friend named after your loved one, it is a blessing.

Q. Can you interpret the practice of naming as a form of reincarnation?

A. Yes, when we name someone who has passed away, it feels like they are reincarnated. For instance, a person leaves us, and then it feels like they came back home. You can get the person's life back through naming. I experienced it myself when I named Rosie after my father. I felt a sense of relief, as if I had gotten my father back in my home. Sulurayok felt the same way, because he really loved his father-in-law. It feels like a reincarnation when you name someone who had passed away.

Nancy Tasseor

Interview Date
August 2012

Q. So when a newborn is named after a lost relative, would the infant be treated as if he or she were actually his or her namesake?

A. When a newborn is named after someone older or deceased, they usually act like their namesake, and are more active. It is like the newborn is fighting for the things that his or her namesake could not do when he or she was alive.

Q. Could anyone do the naming, or was it the responsibility of an elder?

A. Young people today name their children themselves, without asking their parents. It used to be the responsibility of the grandparents to name the infant. Some even have more than one name now.

Q. What happens when someone from outside the immediate family of the deceased names a child after them? For instance, if my father or mother passed away and someone who is not related to me named their child after my mother or father, is it important that I be notified? And how should I react?

A. It is best to ask an elder who knows the rules that Inuit followed back then. Young people in the past were never the ones naming a child. They asked someone who was older, and the older ones would name the children. Nowadays, young people name their children after their best friend, or whoever they like.

Some people now even name their own children after themselves. There is someone from Baker Lake who has a daughter who is named after her. That wasn't the way in the past.

Q. Is it discouraged to name a child after someone who has just recently died? That is, to use a person's name soon after death?

A. In the past it was recommended that someone who had just passed not be named right away. It is totally different today, where people are naming anybody they want and it does not matter if they just passed away.

Q. What about naming dogs? Of course, dogs need names. I suppose they do not get named after humans?

A. I don't know if dogs can be named after humans. One thing I know is that when they named their lead dogs, they did not have long names. Some people give their dogs short names, maybe because it is easier.

Q. How can I tell when a deceased person wishes to have a name in my family?

A. Some Inuit request to be named to a certain family when they know the parents well, even before a child is born. It often happens when an individual becomes sick; they ask a family to be named before they pass away.

Q. Can the opposite also happen? Can an individual be displeased because he or she did not want his or her name placed in a family?

A. I think some Inuit were very honest when they did not want to be named. If an elder does not want to be named in a certain family but is named anyway, the infant will die soon afterwards. It is common for Inuit to give another name to an infant who is constantly sick.

Q. Does naming a child after someone who has passed away help ease the pain of losing a loved one?

A. When a loved one has passed away and a newborn is named after him or her, it makes you feel like you have another chance to live with that person again. Sometimes, when they are not named for a long time, it is hard to forget them, but soon after they are named, it helps to ease the pain.

Q. Can you interpret the practice of naming as a form of reincarnation?

A. Our grandchildren are named after people who were related to my and my husband's parents—our ancestors. My father and my husband's father were the ones who named our older children; that is how it was in the past in our family.